The Believer's Privileges

The Believer's Privileges

by
John MacArthur, Jr.

MOODY PRESS

CHICAGO

All Scripture quotations, unless noted otherwise, are from the *New Ameri-can Standard Bible,* © 1960, 1962, 1963, 1968, 1971, 1972, 1973, 1975, and
1977 by The Lockman Foundation, and are used by permission.

ISBN: 0-8024-5335-X

1 2 3 4 5 6 7 8 Printing/LC/Year 95 94 93 92 91 90

Printed in the United States of America

Contents

These Bible studies are taken from messages delivered by Pastor-Teacher John MacArthur, Jr., at Grace Community Church in Panorama City, California. The recorded messages themselves may be purchased as a series or individually. Please request the current price list by writing to:

"GRACE TO YOU"
P.O. Box 4000
Panorama City, CA 91412

Or call the following toll-free number:
1-800-55-GRACE

1
Union

Outline

Introduction
A. The Theme
   1. The joy of Christian privileges
   2. The meaning of Christian privileges
   3. An illustration of Christian privileges
B. The Text

Lesson
I. The Cornerstone of Our Privileges (v. 4)
  A. The Recipients of the Privileges (v. 4*a*)
    1. They have an established relationship
    2. They have an enduring relationship
  B. The Giver of the Privileges (v. 4*b*)
    1. His identity
    2. His characterizations
      a) The living stone
      b) The foundation stone
      c) The rejected stone
      d) The chosen stone
        (1) He is precious
        (2) He is perfect
      e) The stone of stumbling
II. The Kaleidoscope of Our Privileges (vv. 5-10)
  A. Union (v. 5*a*)
    1. We become pictures of Christ
    2. We become partakers of Christ
    3. We are placed in Christ

Conclusion

Introduction

Peter did not write like Paul. Paul's writing is step by step and is generally easily outlined, but Peter's writing is more cyclical. Peter makes a point, goes on to another point, and then amplifies his first point.

In 1 Peter 2:4-10, Peter weaves in and out of some wonderful truths. In the midst of the revelation he gives us, he repeatedly quotes or alludes to the Old Testament. Peter's knowledge of the Old Testament was apparently so extensive that it came out in his writing almost inadvertently.

A. The Theme

1. The joy of Christian privileges

   The theme of 1 Peter 2:4-10 is spiritual privileges. When we study the Bible we're often studying spiritual duties, exhortations, or commands. But in this passage of Scripture we are neither commanded nor exhorted. Instead, Peter gives us a list explaining what is ours because we are Christ's. This is a passage of great joy for every Christian.

2. The meaning of Christian privileges

   I associate the word *privilege* with my childhood. One of the ways my parents encouraged me to obey was by warning that my disobedience would result in loss of privileges. A privilege is a right or benefit enjoyed beyond the advantages of most others. So the privileged belong to a class that enjoys special favor. That's certainly true of Christians: we enjoy the special favor of spiritual privileges in Christ.

3. An illustration of Christian privileges

   Perhaps the best way to understand the privileges mentioned in verses 4-10 is to look at these verses as if you were gazing into a kaleidoscope. Recently I looked at one that had colored rocks in the end of it, and as I held it up toward the light and turned the end, all kinds of different forms and shapes appeared. But it was always the same rocks, just arranged, magnified, and displayed in different ways. That is a picture of our passage. In 1 Peter 2:4-10, Peter keeps turning the kaleidoscope of Christian privilege. Every time he turns it, you can see the same truths arranged in a panoply of new beauty.

B. The Text

First Peter 2:4-5 says that in coming "to Him [Christ] as to a living stone, rejected by men, but choice and precious in the sight of God, you also, as living stones, are being built up as a spiritual house."

Lesson

I. THE CORNERSTONE OF OUR PRIVILEGES (v. 4)

A. The Recipients of the Privileges (v. 4a)

"Coming to Him."

1. They have an established relationship

It is our coming to Christ that initiates all our spiritual privileges. We often say as Christians that "we came to Christ," and that is is biblical. Jesus calls all men and women to come to Him.

a) Matthew 11:28—"Come to Me, all who are weary and heavy-laden, and I will give you rest."

b) John 6:35—"I am the bread of life; he who comes to Me shall not hunger, and he who believes in Me shall never thirst."

c) John 6:37—"All that the Father gives Me shall come to Me."

d) John 6:44—"No one can come to Me, unless the Father who sent Me draws him."

e) John 6:65—"No one can come to Me, unless it has been granted him from the Father."

f) John 7:37—"If any man is thirsty, let him come to Me and drink."

As one of the disciples present when Jesus taught, Peter had heard Jesus say all those things. He knew from experience that the believer's privileges begin when an individual comes to Christ.

At the moment of salvation, we enter not only the realm of spiritual duty but also the realm of spiritual privilege. Paul affirmed that truth when he said, "Blessed be the God and Father of our Lord Jesus Christ, who has blessed us with every spiritual blessing in the heavenly places in Christ" (Eph. 1:3).

2. They have an enduring relationship

That we came to Christ does not convey Peter's total meaning in this verse. His use of the Greek word *proserchomai* carries the idea not only of coming but also of remaining. The same concept is found in the apostle John's writings, which link our coming to Christ with our abiding in Him (John 15:4-5, 7, 9-10; 1 John 3:24). Peter wanted us to understand that when we come to Christ, a permanent relationship of intimate personal communion is established.

Proserchomai in the Greek translation of the Old Testament was used to speak of drawing near to God for continuing worship. The book of Hebrews speaks of the same idea (Heb. 10:1, 22). *Prosēlutos* (from which we get the word *proselyte*), the Greek noun related to *proserchomai*, refers to a person who was far off but who drew near. In the Bible the word refers to Gentiles—those who were outside God's covenant with Israel and therefore were living outside the law and promises God gave to Israel—who had drawn near and identified with Israel. The proselyte was one who consciously drew near to God's people and remained.

10

Peter's use of words describes the inner movement toward communion with Jesus Christ. That is where our spiritual privileges begin.

B. The Giver of the Privileges (v. 4*b*)

"To a living stone, rejected by men, but choice and precious in the sight of God."

1. His identity

Peter used the analogy of a stone to identify and describe Christ. This first mention of Christ as a stone is the start of an amazing combination of images from three different Old Testament texts that refer to the Messiah as a stone (Isa. 28:16; Ps. 118:22; and Isa. 8:14). Peter used those passages to show that spiritual privilege is based on an abiding relationship to Christ.

The Greek word translated stone (*lithos*, the common word for stone) sometimes spoke of a carved precious stone, but usually meant a stone used in constructing a building—one that was chiseled, hammered, and sawed so that it would fit perfectly. In ancient times buildings were made of stones so heavy and so perfectly fit together that they were simply stacked upon each other and thus were practically immovable.

2. His characterizations

a) The living stone

Peter described that perfectly shaped stone as a "living stone." Now that's a paradoxical statement since we think of a stone as non-living. We sometimes refer to something as "stone dead." But the stone to which Peter referred is a living stone. It has all the solidity of stone, yet is alive. Jesus Christ is that perfect stone, the cornerstone of the church (1 Pet. 2:6). Paul uses similar imagery in 1 Corinthians 10:4, where he says that Christ was the spiritual rock in the wilderness from whom Israel drank (Ex. 17:1-6). It was especially appropriate for Peter to speak of Christ as One who lives because He rose from the dead.

(1) Romans 6:9—"Christ, having been raised from the dead, is never to die again; death no longer is master over Him."

(2) 1 Corinthians 15:45—"The last Adam [Christ] became a life-giving spirit." Not only is Christ alive, but He also gives life to His people.

(3) 1 Peter 1:3—Through Christ, Christians are "born again to a living hope."

(4) 1 Peter 1:23—We are "born again not of seed which is perishable but imperishable, that is, through the living and abiding word of God."

Peter did not say that Christ is "the" stone. He did not use the definite article before the word *lithos*, so the sense of the phrase is, "coming to Him as to living stone." Christ is not one among many stones, but is the stone that possesses life. Anyone who receives Christ by faith is made alive by the life that is in Him. Eternal life is in Christ (1 John 5:11).

b) The foundation stone

Peter used the analogy of a stone to illustrate that Christ is the foundation of the building that is the church. Peter will expand on that theme using Old Testament passages that present Christ in the same way.

c) The rejected stone

Strange as it may seem, the living stone is a rejected stone. That is why so many in this world have no spiritual privileges. They do not enjoy the advantages, favor, and blessings we have because they reject the living stone. When the world rejects the foundation stone of God's church, they reject the only One who can give them life. Peter would have been thinking of the Jewish nation—the Sanhedrin, the leaders, the priests, and the people who followed them—who rejected Jesus Christ, spat upon Him, beat Him, and finally crucified Him. All who reject Him fit into the same category.

Christ: The Perfect Cornerstone

According to the building practices of Peter's time, when men set out to build a building they wanted stones that fit perfectly. The most important stone in the entire building was the cornerstone. The perfection of the cornerstone helped maintain the perfect symmetry of the rest of the building. Like a plumb line stretching in every direction, the cornerstone set the direction lines for the building both horizontally and vertically. If any of the angles were off, the building would be off. If the horizontal angle was not a perfect right angle, the building would be skewed. If the vertical angle was not correct, the building could collapse outward or inward. All those angles were set by one massive cornerstone to which all other stones were laid out in agreement. That is a wonderful picture of how Christ relates to the church.

The leaders of Israel had wanted to participate in the building of God's glorious spiritual Temple. In looking for the Messiah, whom they knew would be the cornerstone of their building, Jesus was presented to them and they examined Him. They measured Christ according to their wisdom and concluded that He was not adequate, so they rejected Him. He did not live up to their calculations. But their calculations were erroneous.

The word Peter uses for rejection embodies the above process because it speaks of rejecting after examination or testing. It was unthinkable to the Jewish leadership that Jesus could possibly be the cornerstone of God's kingdom—a poor and humble man who scathed them with His denunciations of their religious system. So He was sent to die on a cross. He wouldn't overthrow the Romans and establish Israel's freedom, so they rejected Him.

13

d) The chosen stone

   (1) He is precious

   Though He was rejected by men, Jesus was choice
   and precious in the sight of God. Peter's phrasing
   draws a contrast: Christ was rejected in the sight
   of men, but "was choice and precious in the sight
   of God" (1 Pet. 2:4). God measured Christ by the
   measuring instruments of His own perfection,
   and as a result could say, "Thou art My beloved
   Son, in Thee I am well pleased" (Mark 1:11).
   Christ was choice (ordained by God) and precious
   (Gk., *entimon*, "costly," "highly prized," or "rare").

   (2) He is perfect

   In God's estimation, Jesus Christ is the perfect cornerstone, with every angle correct. Because He
   was perfect, Christ was raised from the dead and
   made the living cornerstone of the church.

By Whose Standard Do You Judge Greatness?

I remember reading about a conversation in the Louvre Museum in
Paris. One of the curators of the museum, a man with great appre-
ciation for art, observed two men staring at a masterpiece. One
turned to the other and said, "I don't think much of that painting."
The curator, feeling obliged to reply to the man's statement, said to
him, "Dear sir, if I may interrupt, that painting is not on trial; you
are. The quality of that painting has already been assessed and approved, and you only demonstrate the frailty of your measuring
capability by your judgment." Christ has been approved by God—
it is man who is on trial.

e) The stone of stumbling

   The living stone is perfect and has been approved by
   God. Every man who measures it is on trial to see if
   his system of measuring is adequate. The Jewish people of Peter's day failed to measure correctly as a
   whole, and men and women today continue to reject

the One whom God has declared to be choice and precious.

(1) Psalm 2:12—"Kiss the Son, lest he [God] be angry and you be destroyed in your way" (NIV*).

(2) 1 Corinthians 16:22—"If anyone does not love the Lord [Jesus Christ], let him be accursed."

(3) Acts 2:23-24a—At Pentecost Peter said to his Jewish audience, "You nailed [Christ] to a cross by the hands of godless men and put Him to death. And God raised Him up again." Peter must have loved the subject of Christ's acceptance by the Father because he constantly referred to it.

(4) Acts 2:32-33—"This Jesus God raised up again, to which we are all witnesses. . . . [And He has] been exalted to the right hand of God."

(5) Acts 4:11-12—"The stone which was rejected by you, the builders, . . . became the very corner stone. And there is salvation in no one else."

(6) Acts 5:30-31—"The God of our fathers raised up Jesus, whom you [the Jewish leadership] had put to death by hanging Him on a cross. He is the one whom God exalted to His right hand as a Prince and a Savior."

(7) Acts 10:39-40—"We are witnesses of all the things He did both in the land of the Jews and in Jerusalem. And they also put Him to death by hanging Him on a cross. God raised Him up on the third day, and granted that He should become visible." Although the Jewish people rejected Christ, God affirmed Him.

Men disapproved of Christ at the onset and have continued to do so throughout history. When offered the choice between the sinless Son of God and the murderer Barabbas, the mob chose to crucify Christ and

* *New International Version.*

15

receive Barabbas. There's no better indicator of man's corrupt standards than that. Men still think they can adequately measure Jesus Christ, but their standards are still corrupt. The world despises what God has chosen and hates what God loves most. Therefore the acclaim of the world is worthless—it couldn't even recognize the value of the most precious Person who ever lived.

II. THE KALEIDOSCOPE OF OUR PRIVILEGES (vv. 5-10)

A. Union (v. 5*a*)

"You also, as living stones, are being built up as a spiritual house."

It is from the living stone that we receive our spiritual privileges. Our first look into the kaleidoscope of spiritual privilege shows us the privilege of union with our Lord. We are said to be "living stones."

1. We become pictures of Christ

Christians not only come to the living stone, but they also become living stones themselves. He who comes to Christ becomes like Christ. That is why we are called Christians. It is our privilege to live in accordance with that honorable title. And just as Christ is a living stone, we are being built up as living stones. We have eternal life.

2. We become partakers of Christ

The very life that exists in Christ exists in us. We not only worship, obey, honor, and pray to Him, but are united with Him as well. Christ is the cornerstone, and we are stones who are being built up as a spiritual house. We are part of the same building and possess the same life— it flows from Him to us. That's why Peter said, "He has granted to us His precious and magnificent promises, in order that by them you might become partakers of the divine nature" (2 Pet. 1:4).

16

Christianity is the only religion in which the object of its worship becomes the life of the believer. A Buddhist is not said to be in Buddha. A Confucianist is not in Confucius, or a Muslim in Muhammad. No Buddhists, Confucianists, or Muslims ever taught that they possessed the eternal life of their founder, yet Christians have the life of Christ. We are partakers of the divine nature.

a) Colossians 3:3—Paul said to the Colossian church, "You have died and your life is hidden with Christ in God."

b) Colossians 3:4—Christ "is our life."

c) Galatians 2:20—Paul said, "I have been crucified with Christ; and it is no longer I who live, but Christ lives in me." That is a distinct spiritual privilege. While Christ is our Savior, Redeemer, and God, it is equally true that we share His life. We participate in His eternal nature, obtain the strength of our living stone, possess the same resurrection life, and are built into the same great edifice of which Christ is the cornerstone.

3. We are placed in Christ

Peter said that as living stones, we "are being built up as a spiritual house" (v. 5). God is building that house on the cornerstone of Christ.

a) Ephesians 2:19-22—"You are no longer strangers and aliens, but you are fellow citizens with the saints, and are of God's household, having been built upon the foundation of the apostles and prophets, Christ Jesus Himself being the corner stone, in whom the whole building, being fitted together is growing into a holy temple in the Lord; in whom you also are being built together into a dwelling of God in the Spirit." Christ Himself is the cornerstone of the church, and the remainder of the foundation is the apostles and prophets. Paul was not speaking of personalities but of the doctrine of the apostles and prophets—the Holy Scriptures.

b) Acts 2:42—Those of the early church "were continually devoting themselves to the apostles' teaching." The
foundation of the church is the doctrine that came
through the apostles, and Acts 2 affirms that the early
church studied it. The church was not founded on the
personalities or ministry of the apostles, but on the revealed Word of God that the apostles taught. Christ is
the cornerstone, and apostolic doctrine is based on
Him. As believers are part of the spiritual house being
built on that foundation.

c) 1 Corinthians 3:9—The church is "God's building."

A New House for God

Peter uses strong and vivid language in his description of the
church, especially in light of his upbringing. In the Jewish culture
of his time, Judaism centered on the Temple in Jerusalem—the
earthly, material, temporal house of God. But Peter declared that
in the New Covenant God dwells in a spiritual house—not an
earthly, material, temporal one.

d) Acts 7:48—"The Most High does not dwell in houses
made by human hands."

e) Acts 17:24—"The God who made the world and all
things in it, since He is Lord of heaven and earth,
does not dwell in temples made with hands." God
dwells in a spiritual house made up of Christians,
who are the stones that make up that house.

f) 1 Timothy 3:15—The household of God "is the church
of the living God, the pillar and support of the truth."
God dwells in the hearts of His redeemed people.

g) Hebrews 3:6—"Christ was faithful as a Son over His
[God's] house whose house we are."

Peter presented Christ as the living stone on which the
doctrine of the apostles is laid out as a foundation for the
church. In perfect symmetry God builds the house of His

18

people on that foundation—not on the dead stones of the old Temple but on living people united with Christ.

Peter may have used that picture of God's people due to the circumstances of his readers. It is an appropriate picture since we are the temple of the Holy Spirit (1 Cor. 6:19), who dwells in us both individually and collectively (Eph. 2:22).

Conclusion

The first great spiritual privilege of the believer is union with Christ. He can "do exceeding abundantly beyond all that we ask or think, according to the power that works within us" (Eph. 3:20). We possess spiritual power, having every spiritual resource for every need. That's why Paul said he would not presume to speak of anything except what Christ had accomplished through him (Rom. 16:18).

Because Christ takes up residence in the lives of those who belong to Him, Paul could say that all his spiritual service was "according to His power, which mightily works within me" (Col. 1:29). If you are a Christian, all the good you do is through the resident power within you because of your union with Christ. Christ lives through you, loves through you, speaks through you, serves through you—even worships God through you. The life of Christ in you preserves, controls, conforms, and supplies you. As a Christian, you can truly say, "I have been crucified with Christ; and it is no longer I who live, but Christ lives in me" (Gal. 2:20).

Focusing on the Facts

1. What is the theme of 1 Peter 2:4-10 (see p. 8)?
2. What is meant by the word *privilege* (see p. 8)?
3. What initiates the rights of spiritual privilege (1 Pet. 2:4; see pp. 9-10)?
4. The Greek word *proserchomai* not only contains the idea of coming to Christ but also the idea of _____ (see p. 10).
5. Which Old Testament texts describe Christ as a stone? Why did Peter use that description of Christ (see p. 11)?

6. What other New Testament writer described Christ as a stone? Where (see p. 11)?
7. Why can it be said of Christ that He is a living stone (see pp. 11-12)?
8. What is the result of rejecting the living stone (see pp. 12-13)?
9. How is the picture of Christ as a stone a metaphor for Christ's relationship to the church (see p. 12)?
10. What does the world's rejection of Christ imply about the value of worldly acclaim (see pp. 15-16)?
11. Christians not only come to the living stone, but also become _____ _____ (see p. 16).
12. What is unique about Christianity in comparison to the world's religions (see pp. 16-17)?
13. What is different about the temples of the New and Old Covenants (see. p. 18)?
14. What do believers possess by virtue of their union with Christ (see p. 19)?

Pondering the Principles

1. The church of our day tends to rely on self-generated programs rather than the life generated from Christ to us. Though the Christian life is to be a continual coming to Christ for renewal and refreshment, we too often turn to broken cisterns that contain no water. Commenting on the text of 1 Peter 2:4-5 more than a hundred years ago, British pastor Charles Haddon Spurgeon exhorted his people to avoid the same error: "God grant us the grace to realize as a church that we are the temple of God, and realize it best by coming daily to Christ more and more closely, that we may be vitally one with Him" (*The Treasury of the Bible*, vol. 4 [London: Marshall, Morgan and Scott, 1963], p. 380). Examine how you spend your time. Is your life characterized by a continual coming to and abiding in Christ? Is it time for you to reorganize your hours so that you can drink deeply from God's Word and enjoy His companionship in prayer?

2. A house is generally a reflection of the characteristics and tastes of its owner. That is even more true if the owner designed and built the house himself—sparing no expense in the process. And that is no less true of God's dwelling-place. Puritan Thomas Watson put it well when he said, "Christ never admired anything but the beauty of holiness: he slighted the glorious

buildings of the temple, but admired the woman's faith. . . . The Lord has two heavens to dwell in, and the holy heart is one of them" (*A Body of Divinity* [Edinburgh: Banner of Truth, 1978 reprint], p. 248). Christians are to furnish themselves in such a way that they reflect their owner's tastes. Whose tastes do you reflect?

2
Access—Part 1

Outline

Review
I. The Cornerstone of Our Privileges (v. 4)
II. The Kaleidoscope of Our Privileges (vv. 5-10)
   A. Union (v. 5*a*)

Lesson
   B. Access (v. 5*b*)
      1. The privileged people
         a) As compared to other religions
         b) As highlighted in the New Testament
            (1) The Old Testament restriction
               (*a*) An impure priesthood
               (*b*) A restricted priesthood
            (2) The New Testament reality
      2. The priestly purpose
         a) The makeup of a priest
            (1) Priests are elect
               (*a*) The Old Testament precedent
               (*b*) The New Testament parallel
            (2) Priests are specially cleansed
               (*a*) The Old Testament precedent
               (*b*) The New Testament parallel
            (3) Priests are specially clothed
               (*a*) The Old Testament precedent
               (*b*) The New Testament parallel
            (4) Priests are anointed
               (*a*) The Old Testament precedent
               (*b*) The New Testament parallel

       (5)   Priests are specially prepared
           (*a*) The Old Testament precedent
           (*b*) The New Testament parallel
       (6)   Priests are ordained to obedience
           (*a*) The Old Testament precedent
           (*b*) The New Testament parallel
       (7)   Priests love God's Word
       (8)   Priests walk with God
       (9)   Priests have an impact on sinners
     (10)   Priests are God's messengers

Conclusion

Review

I. THE CORNERSTONE OF OUR PRIVILEGES (v. 4; see pp. 9-16)

II. THE KALEIDOSCOPE OF OUR PRIVILEGES (vv. 5-10)

   A. Union (v. 5*a*; see pp. 16-19)

Lesson

   B. Access (v. 5*b*)

"[Believers] are being built up as a spiritual house for a holy priesthood, to offer up spiritual sacrifices acceptable to God through Jesus Christ."

1. The privileged people

   a) As compared to other religions

Christians enjoy not only union with their Lord, but also admission to His presence. That is a rare privilege not enjoyed by the masses of unredeemed people. Because those masses are far from Him and do not know Him, the Bible says they are unwelcome in His presence.

That barrier between God and man is reflected in the world's religions. The various deities man invents are remote, indifferent, and apathetic to human needs and problems. Man is willing to appease his idols, but he does not desire to draw near to them. Rather, he greatly fears them.

b) As highlighted in the New Testament

(1) The Old Testament restriction

In the Old Testament we see that the average Jew could pray to God and draw into His presence spiritually, but he did not have access to Him physically. Before God came down on Mount Sinai, He warned the people not to come near or even touch the mountain. No one but the high priest was allowed to enter God's presence—and that only once a year in the Holy of Holies in the Temple.

(a) An impure priesthood

When the high priest entered God's presence on the Day of Atonement, it was such a sacred event that he had to go through a ceremonial washing, make a spiritual confession, and offer a sacrifice for his own sin to make sure he was clean before God.

(b) A restricted priesthood

Old Testament law restricted the offering of sacrifices to the priesthood. Anyone who attempted to usurp the office of a priest was in danger of severe judgment. God afflicted King Azariah (also called Uzziah) with leprosy for doing just that (2 Kings 15:5; 2 Chron. 26:16-21). King Saul tried to function like a priest, so God cursed his lineage, promising that no king would come from his loins (1 Sam. 13:8-14). When Korah and his rebellious followers attempted to act as priests, the ground opened and swallowed them (Num. 16).

25

(2) The New Testament reality

What was limited in the Old Covenant to the high priest is the unlimited opportunity and privilege of every Christian. According to 1 Peter 2:5, believers are both the Temple of God and the priests who serve in it.

What is more, verse 9 says that we are a royal priesthood. As a chosen race and holy nation, we are given access to God.

2. The priestly purpose

Although we acknowledge that we are priests and therefore have access to God, many don't really know what a priest is. So we need to examine the Old Testament priesthood to understand our position as priests.

Under the Old Covenant the priest's main job was to offer acceptable sacrifices to God, and so it is with us. First Peter 2:5 says we're "to offer up spiritual sacrifices acceptable to God through Jesus Christ."

a) The makeup of a priest

There are three passages in the Old Testament that, when combined, give us a good picture of the makeup of a priest: Exodus 28-29, Leviticus 8-9, and Malachi 2. Exodus 28-29 lays out God's standards for the priesthood—the office is defined and its functions are described. Leviticus 8-9 contains the inauguration of the priesthood. Malachi 2 was written much later. It helps to define the priesthood by comparing the apostate priesthood of Malachi's time with the true priesthood instituted in the time of Moses. In those passages we see ten characteristics of a priest, and they parallel the nature and features of the believer's priesthood.

(1) Priests are elect

(a) The Old Testament precedent

According to Exodus 28, God chooses His priests. In verse 1 God says to Moses, "Bring near to yourself Aaron your brother, and his sons with him, from among the sons of Israel, to minister as priests to Me—Aaron, Nadab and Abihu, Eleazar and Ithamar, Aaron's sons." No one volunteered for the priesthood. There weren't any applications to fill out and file with Moses. No one voted on who the priests would be. No spiritual or intellectual aptitude tests were given. God sovereignly chose Aaron, Nadab, Abihu, Eleazar, Ithamar, and their descendants to serve as priests.

Levi: God's Unusual Choice

Aaron and his sons were of the tribe of Levi. That was the tribe in Israel from which all the priests were chosen. But that entire tribe had been cursed by Jacob, Levi's father: "Simeon and Levi are brothers; their swords are implements of violence. Let my soul not enter into their council; let not my glory be united with their assembly; because in their anger they slew men, and in their self-will they lamed oxen" (Gen. 49:5-6). Levi was a violent man. When he and Simeon lamed the oxen, they were destroying the owner's ability to feed his family. Genesis 34 records how Levi and Simeon slaughtered the men of an entire city. Jacob said later, "Cursed be their anger, for it is fierce; and their wrath, for it is cruel. I will disperse them in Jacob, and scatter them in Israel" (Gen. 49:7).

The Lord chose His priests from a tribe that was known for its cursedness, violence, and sinfulness. Levi was a tribe of the morally feeble and was probably one of the least respected in Israel. Yet it was from that very tribe that God chose the Old Testament priests.

(b) The New Testament parallel

Our priesthood is also an elect priesthood. Jesus said to His disciples, "You did not choose Me, but I chose you" (John 15:16). We are the elect of God who were chosen in Christ before the foundation of the world (Eph. 1:4). In God's sight the only true priests today are Christians, and all true Christians are priests.

God's unusual choice of Levi and the Old Testament priesthood has a parallel in the New Testament:

(i) Luke 5:32—Jesus said, "I have not come to call the righteous but sinners to repentance."

(ii) Hebrews 7:28—"The Law appoints men as high priests who are weak." Under the Old Covenant God's chosen priests were weak. And God is still choosing the same kind of people. Isn't it wonderful that we who were weak and cursed with sin have been chosen to be priests of the Most High God?

(iii) 1 Corinthians 1:26-29—"Consider your calling, brethren, that there were not many wise according to the flesh, not many mighty, not many noble; but God has chosen the foolish things of the world to shame the wise, and God has chosen the weak things of the world to shame the things which are strong, and the base things of the world and the despised, God has chosen, the things that are not, that He might nullify the things that are, that no man should boast before God." God continues to choose His priests from among the lowly, just as He chose Aaron of the tribe of Levi.

(2) Priests are specially cleansed

(a) The Old Testament precedent

Before a priest could begin his ministry, he needed to be cleansed from sin. Leviticus 8:6 says that "Moses had Aaron and his sons come near, and washed them with water." That was an outward symbol of their inward need. Next Moses "put the tunic on [Aaron] and girded him with the sash, and clothed him with the robe, and put the ephod [apron] on him; and he girded him with the artistic band of the ephod, with which he tied it to him. He then placed the breastpiece on him, and in the breastpiece he put the Urim and the Thummim [by which God could reveal His will]. He also placed the turban on his head, and on the turban, at its front, he placed the golden plate, the holy crown, just as the Lord had commanded Moses.

"Moses then . . . poured some of the anointing oil on Aaron's head and anointed him, to consecrate him. Next Moses had Aaron's sons come near and clothed them with tunics, and girded them with sashes, and bound caps on them, just as the Lord had commanded Moses.

"Then he brought the bull of the sin offering, and Aaron and his sons laid their hands on the head of the bull of the sin offering. Next Moses slaughtered it" (vv. 7-15). First Aaron and his sons needed to be washed with water, then they were anointed with oil, and finally their sins were atoned for with blood. All that represented their need to be cleansed from sin.

Moses then "presented the ram of the burnt offering. . . . Then he presented the second ram, the ram of ordination; and Aaron and his sons laid their hands on the head of the ram. And Moses slaughtered it and took some of its blood and put it on the lobe of Aaron's right ear, and on the thumb of his right hand, and on the big toe of his right foot. He also had Aaron's sons come near; and Moses put some of the blood on the lobe of their right ear, and on the thumb of their right hand, and on the big toe of their right foot.

"Moses then sprinkled the rest of the blood around on the altar. And he took the fat, and the fat tail, and all the fat that was on the entrails, and the lobe of the liver and the two kidneys and their fat and the right thigh. And from the basket of unleavened bread that was before the Lord, he took one unleavened cake and one cake of bread mixed with oil and one wafer, and placed them on the portions of fat and on the right thigh. He then put all these on the hands of Aaron and on the hands of his sons, and presented them as a wave offering before the Lord. Then Moses took them from their hands and offered them up in smoke on the altar with the burnt offering. They were an ordination offering for a soothing aroma; it was an offering by fire to the Lord. . . .

"Moses took some of the anointing oil and some of the blood which was on the altar, and sprinkled it on Aaron, on his garments, on his sons, and on the garments of his sons with him; and he consecrated Aaron, his garments, and his sons, and the garments of his sons with him" (vv. 18-30).

The washing, anointing, and all the offerings demonstrated that a priest could not function until he was fully cleansed—from top to bottom, ear to toe. The blood on his right ear was apparently to sanctify his ear for hearing the Word of God, the blood on his right thumb to sanctify his hands for the work of God, and the blood on his right toe to sanctify his feet for walking with God.

(b) The New Testament parallel

Like the Old Testament priests, we could not be called priests if we had not been cleansed from our sin.

  (i) Titus 2:14—Christ "gave Himself for us, that He might redeem us from every lawless deed and purify for Himself a people for His own possession, zealous for good deeds."

  (ii) Titus 3:5—"He saved us not on the basis of deeds which we have done in righteousness, but according to His mercy, by the washing of regeneration and renewing by the Holy Spirit."

  (iii) Ephesians 5:26—Christ washed us "with the Word."

  (iv) 1 Peter 1:2—Christ sprinkled us "with His blood."

(3) Priests are specially clothed

(a) The Old Testament precedent

Once a priest was cleansed from sin, he was then clothed for service. In Exodus 28:42 Moses was instructed to make linen undershorts for the priests, which apparently symbolized sexual purity. As we learned from Leviticus 8 a priest also wore a tunic, a belt, a robe, and an ephod including a decorative band. A breastpiece went over the ephod and a turban was placed on the priest's head, with a golden plate at the front of the turban. All those special garments symbolized the unique call of a priest to virtue and identification with God.

31

(*b*) The New Testament parallel

Psalm 132:9 says, "Let Thy priests be clothed with righteousness." As a Christian you are a priest who has been clothed with the righteousness of Christ, for as 1 Corinthians 1:30 says, "You are in Christ Jesus, who became to us wisdom from God, and righteousness and sanctification, and redemption."

(4) Priests are anointed

(*a*) The Old Testament precedent

Leviticus 8 tells us that the priests were anointed. Verse 12 shows Moses pouring oil on Aaron's head. Verse 30 describes Moses taking some of the anointing oil from the altar and sprinkling it on Aaron and his garments, and on his sons and their garments. That identified the priesthood as the special class on whom the power and presence of God would rest. The anointing oil symbolized God's Spirit.

(*b*) The New Testament parallel

Similarly, New Testament believers are anointed by the Holy Spirit:

(i) 1 John 2:20—The apostle John said to believers, "You have an anointing from the Holy One."

(ii) 1 John 2:27—"The anointing which you received from Him abides in you." Who abides in the believer? The Holy Spirit. The Christian's body is the temple of the Holy Spirit (1 Cor. 3:16).

The anointing of the Spirit gives power. Acts 1:8 says, "You shall receive power when the Holy Spirit has come upon you." The priests in the Old Testament could do what nobody else could do, go where no one else could go, and act in ways that no one else could act. Their special authority, privileges, rights, and powers have been granted to New Testament believers by the anointing of the Spirit.

(5) Priests are specially prepared

(a) The Old Testament precedent

The priests were not just anointed and empowered for service; they were also specially prepared for it. After all the preparation we have seen so far, Leviticus 8:33 adds, "And you shall not go outside the doorway of the tent of meeting for seven days, until the day that the period of your ordination is fulfilled; for he will ordain you through seven days."

After the seven days the priests were instructed to give special offerings that would prepare them for their office (Lev. 9:4). Then "Moses and Aaron went into the tent of meeting. When they came out and blessed the people, the glory of the Lord appeared to all the people. Then fire came out from before the Lord and consumed the burnt offering and the portions of fat on the altar; and when all the people saw it, they shouted and fell on their faces" (Lev. 9:23-24).

Before a person could actually function as a priest, his heart needed to be prepared. Those seven days were symbolic of spiritual preparedness—the readiness of mind and heart for the seriousness of priesthood.

(b) The New Testament parallel

Similarly, every believer should seriously consider the great privileges and responsibilities of spiritual service. When a person makes a profession of faith in Jesus Christ, the Spirit of

God usually ripens the marvelous gift of salvation before the believer is ready for spiritual ministry. That time of preparation readies the heart of the believer for priestly service.

(6) Priests are ordained to obedience

(a) The Old Testament precedent

Leviticus 10 is one of the saddest portions of Scripture—a tragic account of priestly disobedience. There we see two newly called, cleansed, clothed, anointed, and prepared priests embarking upon their ministry. Fire had come out from the Lord's presence at the end of their seven days of preparation and burned up their sacrifices. The account continues: "Nadab and Abihu, the sons of Aaron, took their respective firepans, and after putting fire in them, placed incense on it and offered strange fire before the Lord, which He had not commanded them. And fire came out from the presence of the Lord and consumed them, and they died before the Lord" (vv. 1-2).

Can you imagine the shock? The entire assembly witnessed that event. Aaron must have been stunned, but Moses explained, "It is what the Lord spoke, saying, 'By those who come near Me I will be treated as holy, and before all the people I will be honored' " (v. 3). The message was clear: every priest is ordained to obedience. Those who have the privilege of coming near to God must regard Him as holy.

(b) The New Testament parallel

New Testament believers are called to the same priestly obedience. Peter said, "As obedient children, do not be conformed to the former lusts which were yours in your ignorance" (1 Pet. 1:14).

(7) Priests love God's Word

God's priests were to have a high regard for the Word of God.

(*a*) Malachi 2:1-8—The prophet Malachi indicted the apostate priesthood of his time by measuring them against the God-ordained principles given through Moses: " 'This commandment is for you, O priests. If you do not listen, if you do not take it to heart to give honor to My name,' says the Lord of hosts, 'then I will send the curse upon you, and I will curse your blessings; and indeed, I have cursed them already, because you are not taking it to heart. Behold, I am going to rebuke your offspring, and I will spread refuse on your faces, the refuse of your feasts; and you will be taken away with it. Then you will know that I have sent this commandment to you, that My covenant may continue with Levi,' says the Lord of hosts" (vv. 1-4).

Looking back to the beginning of that covenant, the Lord said through Malachi, "My covenant with him was one of life and peace, and I gave them to him as an object of reverence; so he revered Me, and stood in awe of My name. True instruction was in his mouth, and unrighteousness was not found on his lips; he walked with Me in peace and uprightness, and he turned many back from iniquity. For the lips of a priest should preserve knowledge, and men should seek instruction from his mouth; for he is the messenger of the Lord of hosts. But as for you, you have turned aside from the way; you have caused many to stumble by the instruction; you have corrupted the covenant of Levi" (vv. 5-8).

(*b*) Exodus 32:26-28—This text illustrates how seriously the early priests took the Word of God. Moses had gone up into the mountain to receive the law, and when he returned, the people were worshiping a golden calf. "Moses stood in the gate of the camp, and said, 'Whoever is for the Lord, come to me!' And all the sons of Levi gathered together to him. And he said to them, 'Thus says the Lord, the God of Israel, "Every man of you put his sword upon his thigh, and go back and forth from gate to gate in the camp, and kill every man his brother, and every man his friend, and every man his neighbor." ' So the sons of Levi did as Moses instructed, and about three thousand men of the people fell that day." In the beginning the priests took the Word of God seriously, and that is the standard to which Malachi pointed when he rebuked the priesthood of his own day.

(c) Deuteronomy 33:10—Of the tribe of Levi Moses said, "They shall teach Thine ordinances to Jacob, and Thy Law to Israel." From the beginning God designed the priesthood to be faithful to His Word.

(d) Numbers 25:10-13—"The Lord spoke to Moses, saying, 'Phinehas the son of Eleazar, the son of Aaron the priest, has turned away My wrath from the sons of Israel, in that he was jealous with My jealousy among them, so that I did not destroy the sons of Israel in My jealousy. Therefore say, "Behold, I give him My covenant of peace; and it shall be for him and his descendants after him, a covenant of a perpetual priesthood." ' " When Malachi referred to the Lord's covenant "with him" (Mal. 2:5), he was probably speaking of Phinehas. Phinehas was a zealous priest and is an emblem of a godly priesthood who takes the Word of God seriously.

(8) Priests walk with God

A priest walked with God. Malachi 2:6 says of God's priest, "He walked with Me in peace and uprightness."

(9) Priests have an impact on sinners

Malachi also affirmed that a priest was to have a positive impact on sinners. The priesthood to which Malachi was referring "turned many back from iniquity" (Mal. 2:6).

(10) Priests are God's messengers

A priest was to be the Lord's messenger: "The lips of a priest should preserve knowledge, and men should seek instruction from his mouth; for he is the messenger of the Lord of hosts" (Mal. 2:7).

Conclusion

How do the qualifications of the Old Testament priesthood relate to the New Testament believer? First Peter 2:5 says that we are priests. As priests we are chosen, cleansed, clothed with righteousness, anointed with the Holy Spirit, prepared for service, and ordained to obedience. We are to highly regard the Word of God, walk with God, impact sinners, and act as messengers of the Lord. That was true of the Old Testament priesthood, and it is also true of us.

Focusing on the Facts

1. Who enjoys the privilege of access to God (see p. 24)?
2. Explain the different means of access to God allowed under the Old and New Covenants (see pp. 25-26).
3. In the Old Testament era, what steps were necessary before the High Priest entered the Temple (see p. 25)?
4. Old Testament law restricted the offering of sacrifices _____ _____ _____ (see p. 25).
5. What three Old Testament passages, when combined, give us a picture of the makeup of a priest? What is the emphasis of each passage (see p. 26)?
6. Who appointed God's priests (Ex. 28:1; see p. 27)?

7. What similarities exist between those chosen for the priesthood from the tribe of Levi and those God now chooses as priests (see pp. 27-28)?
8. Before an Old Testament priest could begin his ministry, he needed to be _____ (see p. 29).
9. In what way has Christ cleansed us for priestly service (see p. 31)?
10. In the Old Testament the priests were specially clothed. What is the special clothing of a believer's priesthood (see p. 32)?
11. New Testament believers have been anointed by _____ _____ (see pp. 32-33).
12. What did Old Testament priests need in addition to empowerment and anointing (see p. 33)?
13. What does Leviticus 10:1-2 show us that God's priests are ordained to (see p. 34)?
14. What does Malachi 2 teach us about four intended functions of the priest (see pp. 35-37)?

Pondering the Principles

1. One thing believers enjoy as priests is access to God. Thomas Watson wrote, "God has made His children, by adoption, nearer to Himself than the angels. The angels are the friends of Christ; believers are His members" (cited in *A Puritan Golden Treasury*, I. D. E. Thomas, ed. [Edinburgh: Banner of Truth, 1977], p. 50). A relationship of intimacy involves both the privilege of access and enjoyment as well as the responsibility of conforming one's behavior and thinking to further that relationship. As you consider the privileges that are yours as a believer-priest, how are you encouraged to further your relationship with God?

2. What we have learned about a priest's makeup affirms that God's priests are a people set apart to reflect His character. Thomas Watson also said, "It is one of the saddest sights to see a man lift up his hands in prayer, and with those hands oppress; to hear the same tongue praise God at one time, and at another lie and slander; to hear a man in words profess God, and in works deny Him. Oh, how unworthy is this!" (*All Things for Good* [Edinburgh: Banner of Truth, 1986], p. 120). As people

who come from God's very presence we serve as God's representatives. What kind of God do you represent to those who know you? What can you do to allow others to see God more clearly in you?

3
Access—Part 2

Outline

Introduction

Review
 I. The Cornerstone of Our Privileges (v. 4)
 II. The Kaleidoscope of Our Privileges (vv. 5-10)
   A. Union (v. 5*a*)
   B. Access (v. 5*b*)
    1. The privileged people
    2. The priestly purpose
      a) The makeup of a priest

Lesson
      b) The mission of a priest
        (1) The Old Testament precedent
          (*a*) The priestly office
          (*b*) The priestly offering
          (*c*) The priestly right
        (2) The New Testament parallel
          (*a*) Spiritual sacrifice involves the whole person
          (*b*) Spiritual sacrifice involves constant praise
          (*c*) Spiritual sacrifice involves good works
          (*d*) Spiritual sacrifice involves the giving of gifts
          (*e*) Spiritual sacrifice involves reaching the lost
          (*f*) Spiritual sacrifice involves love
          (*g*) Spiritual sacrifice involves prayer

Conclusion

Introduction

Christians live in the confidence that God blesses His people. When we are faithful to Him, He honors us. God does not miss His target when He blesses or judges. Ephesians 1:3 declares that God "has blessed us with every spiritual blessing in the heavenly places in Christ." Galatians 3:9 says, "Those who are of faith are blessed."

Review

I. THE CORNERSTONE OF OUR PRIVILEGES (v. 4; pp. 9-16)

II. THE KALEIDOSCOPE OF OUR PRIVILEGES (vv. 5-10)

    A. Union (v. 5*a*; pp. 16-19)

    B. Access (v. 5*b*; pp. 24-37)

        "[Believers] are being built up as a spiritual house for a holy priesthood, to offer up spiritual sacrifices acceptable to God through Jesus Christ."

        1. The privileged people (pp. 24-26)

        2. The priestly purpose

            a) The makeup of a priest (pp. 26-37)

Lesson

            b) The mission of a priest

                As believers it is important that we understand not only who we are as priests, but also what our function is.

(1) The Old Testament precedent

(a) The priestly office

The function of the Old Testament priesthood was to offer animal and other sacrifices to God. Animal sacrifices ceased to have meaning after the sacrifice of Jesus Christ on the cross; therefore Peter said that the sacrifices now to be offered are spiritual sacrifices. Similarly, God's priesthood is no longer selected from the tribe of Levi through the loins of Aaron. It is a spiritual priesthood made up of believers in Jesus Christ.

(b) The priestly offering

The Old Testament priests knew that any sacrifices offered to God had to be acceptable. For example, any lamb offered had to be the best—without blemish. The sacrifice itself had to be offered in such a way that it violated none of God's commands. Aaron's sons lost their lives when they offered sacrifices in an unacceptable manner. Christians also are responsible for offering sacrifices that are acceptable to God.

(c) The priestly right

Not every sacrifice offered to God was acceptable. King Saul made a sacrifice, contrary to God's express command through Samuel (1 Sam. 10:8; 13:8-14). God cursed Saul's entire line, rejecting both Saul and his heirs for the kingship of Israel.

(2) The New Testament parallel

The purpose of a believer's spiritual sacrifices is to receive God's approval. Believers are to offer "spiritual sacrifices acceptable to God through Jesus Christ'' (1 Pet. 2:5). Because Christ is the sole mediator between God and man (1 Tim. 2:5), we must offer our sacrifices in His name, which means they must be consistent with His will for God to be pleased.

In John 14:12-14 Jesus says, "I go to the Father. . . . Whatever you ask in My name, that will I do, that the Father may be glorified in the Son. If you ask Me anything in My name, I will do it." The key phrase in Jesus' statement is "whatever you ask in My name." That means that whatever a believer asks for must be consistent with who Christ is—His will, His plan, and His kingdom.

A believer's offering to God must be consistent with the Person and work of Christ. It must fit into His plan and be conformed to His design as revealed in the Word of God. It must be a pure sacrifice, springing out of pure motives and extending toward a pure goal. The believer's goal is to honor God. All his actions are to honor God.

For a believer's spiritual sacrifices to honor God they must conform to His Word. This is what the Word specifies:

(*a*) Spiritual sacrifice involves the whole person

   (i) Romans 12—This is the beginning of the application section of that great epistle. In verse 1 Paul says, "I urge you therefore, brethren, by the mercies of God [that which God has mercifully done for believers as recorded in Rom. 1-11], to present your bodies a living and holy sacrifice, acceptable to God, which is your spiritual service of worship." When combined with Peter's wording in 1 Peter 2:5, the idea of the two verses is, "Because of God's mercy toward you, you are now a holy priesthood, and the Lord wants you to offer up spiritual sacrifices. Therefore you must start your priestly work by presenting yourselves as a living and holy sacrifice."

Believers are priests involved in the spiritual service of worship. That service begins with the presentation of our bodies as a living and holy sacrifice. The term "body" obviously includes the mind because Romans 12:2 says, "Do not be conformed to this world, but be transformed by the renewing of your mind, that you may prove what the will of God is, that which is good and acceptable and perfect." All your faculties—your feet, hands, mind, eyes, mouth, ears—are to be used for God's glory.

(ii) Romans 6—The apostle Paul said to the Roman church that before they were saved, their members—bodily parts— were slaves to sin (v. 13). But when they believed they became slaves of righteousness (v. 18). Every part of the believer's body is to be given in sacrifice to God for holy purposes.

(iii) 1 Corinthians 9—Paul said, "I buffet my body and make it my slave" (v. 27). Paul disciplined himself that he might present all his faculties to God. As priests, we do not present dead animals to God, but we give Him our live selves—all that we are. God wants a living sacrifice.

(iv) Hebrews 11—The classic illustration of a living sacrifice is Abraham. Abraham took Isaac to Mount Moriah because God told him to take his son and offer him as a sacrifice. Just as Abraham lifted his knife to plunge it into Isaac's heart, God stopped him and provided a ram as a substitute sacrifice. If Abraham had killed his son, Isaac would have been a dead sacrifice.

That would have been a painful thing for Abraham to do, but Abraham would have been made a living sacrifice because in killing Isaac, he would have sacrificed all his personal hopes and dreams. By slaying Isaac, Abraham would have sacrificed the promises that God had given to him—that his descendants would be "as the stars of heaven in number, and innumerable as the sand which is by the seashore" (v. 12).

Believers are not to offer God something that is dead. We are to offer everything we are, everything we have, and everything we hope to be—all our dreams, hopes, aspirations, and abilities. That's the kind of sacrifice New Testament believers are called to make.

(b) Spiritual sacrifice involves constant praise

Hebrews 13:15 says to us New Covenant priests, "Through Him [Christ] . . . let us continually offer up a sacrifice of praise to God, that is, the fruit of lips that give thanks to His name." Praise is an offering that God requires of His priests.

(i) Reciting God's attributes

In the Old Testament, praising God typically centered on reciting God's glorious attributes. The psalms have many examples of that kind of praise. To cite just one, Psalm 104 says, "Bless the Lord, O my soul! O Lord my God, Thou art very great; Thou art clothed with splendor and majesty, covering Thyself with light as with a cloak" (vv. 1-2). Praise is reciting God's attributes from the heart—exalting Him for His wisdom and knowledge, and honoring and revering God for who He is.

(ii) Reciting God's works

God is great not only for who He is but also for what He has done. If there were no other reason for studying the Old Testament, its record of God's works would be enough. Praise is not merely repeating the phrase "praise the Lord" over and over again. It is exalting God by reciting His attributes and works.

Christians should be relentless in praising God. If you are a Christian, your entire being should be filled with praise and thanksgiving. That is an acceptable spiritual sacrifice. The Christian life isn't defined by how often you go to church, which functions you attend, the number of Christian cassettes you have, or the seminars you have attended. True spiritual life means that you have given all your faculties as a living sacrifice to God to do with as He chooses.

(c) Spiritual sacrifice involves good works

Hebrews 13:16 directs us "not [to] neglect doing good . . . for with such sacrifices God is pleased." We are to do good, which is the opposite of sin, and thereby honor God through our conduct. When you do good in word or deed by offering reproof, restoration, love, and help, you are offering a spiritual sacrifice in the name of Christ that glorifies God.

(d) Spiritual sacrifice involves the giving of gifts

(i) Hebrews 13:16—"Do not neglect . . . sharing; for with such sacrifices God is pleased." That means sharing your resources to meet the needs of someone else.

(ii) Philippians 4:10-18—When Paul wrote to the Philippians, he was a prisoner in

47

Rome. Because they loved Paul, they sent him support, and these verses record his gratitude: "I rejoiced in the Lord greatly, that . . . you have revived your concern for me; indeed, you were concerned before, but you lacked opportunity. Not that I speak from want; for I have learned to be content in whatever circumstances I am. I know how to get along with humble means, and I also know how to live in prosperity; in any and every circumstance I have learned the secret of being filled and going hungry, both of having abundance and suffering need. I can do all things through Him who strengthens me" (vv. 10-13).

This passage is not only a lesson in gratitude, but also a lesson in sharing. Even though Paul didn't need the gift, he said to the Philippians, "Nevertheless, you have done well to share with me in my affliction. And you yourselves also know, Philippians, that at the first preaching of the gospel, after I departed from Macedonia, no church shared with me in the matter of giving and receiving but you alone; for even in Thessalonica you sent a gift more than once for my needs. Not that I seek the gift itself, but I seek for the profit which increases to your account" (vv. 14-17). God blesses the generous, and Paul was glad that the Philippians had put themselves in a position to be blessed. He was especially pleased because their gift was an "acceptable sacrifice, well-pleasing to God" (v. 18).

What About Me?

Our response to the needs of others is often something like, "If I give to them, what will happen when I am in need? Who will take care of my needs?" In Philippians 4:19 Paul says, "God shall supply all your needs according to His riches in glory in Christ Jesus." Nothing makes a pastor more joyful than to see his beloved church offering up spiritual sacrifices acceptable to God, functioning as a holy priesthood, and thereby entering into the place of blessing (vv. 16-18). Paul could rejoice because he knew that the same God who had met all his needs would meet the needs of the generous believer.

(e) Spiritual sacrifice involves reaching the lost

In Romans 15:16 Paul says, "[I am] a minister of Christ Jesus to the Gentiles, ministering as a priest the gospel of God, that my offering of the Gentiles might become acceptable, sanctified by the Holy Spirit." Paul viewed the souls he had been privileged to lead to Christ as an offering to God. We should be able to say with Paul, "Lord Jesus, this friend (neighbor, classmate, or relative) is my sacrifice to You. Thank You for using me as Your instrument in leading this person to Christ."

(f) Spiritual sacrifice involves love

Ephesians 5:2 says, "Walk in love, just as Christ also loved you, and gave Himself up for us, an offering and a sacrifice to God as a fragrant aroma." Christ's love for us resulted in the sacrifice of Himself—and that was a sacrifice acceptable to God. We are to exhibit the humility of Christ. That kind of sacrificial love for one another is well pleasing to God.

(g) Spiritual sacrifice involves prayer

In Revelation 8:3 we see that prayer is a spiritual sacrifice: "Another angel came and stood at the altar, holding a golden censer; and much incense was given to him, that he might add it to the prayers of all the saints upon the golden altar which was before the throne. And the smoke of the incense, with the prayers of the saints, went up before God."

49

Conclusion

Spiritual sacrifice begins when we offer everything we are to God. Praise, good works, generosity, evangelism, love, and prayer are all sacrifices that should follow that initial offering of one's self to God. They are all a sweet aroma in the nostrils of God. As a royal priesthood, it is our privilege to offer up those spiritual sacrifices.

To gather together as a church is not our end goal. Unless we go out from fellowship and instruction in the Word to offer up spiritual sacrifices, we fail in both our worship and our response to worship.

Focusing on the Facts

1. What was the function of the priests in the Old Testament (see p. 43)?
2. Why is it no longer necessary to offer animal sacrifices to God (see p. 43)?
3. A believer's offering to God must be consistent with the _____ and _____ of Christ (see p. 44).
4. What is necessary for a believer's spiritual sacrifices to be honoring to God (see p. 44)?
5. Where does our spiritual service begin (see p. 45)?
6. What does Romans 12:2 confirm regarding the mind's role in spiritual sacrifice (see p. 45)?
7. Believers are not to offer God something that is dead. What are we to offer Him (see p. 46)?
8. What is praise (see pp. 46-47)?
9. What is true spiritual life (see p. 47)?
10. What does the Bible say about giving as a spiritual sacrifice (see pp. 47-48)?
11. How did Paul view the souls he was privileged to bring to Christ (Rom. 15:16; see p. 49)?
12. Does love involve sacrifice? Explain (see p. 49).

Pondering the Principles

1. In a society that advocates freedom from responsibility we often forget that all privileges have corresponding duties. In the seventeenth century Samuel Bolton wrote, "All delight in duties arises from a suitability of spirit in the doing of them. If there is no grace within the heart to answer to the call of duty from without, if there is no principle in the heart agreeable to the precept of the Word, the heart will never delight in them. This, then, is the reason why a godly man conducts himself well in duty, not merely because it is commanded, but because he has the nature which truly and rightly responds to the command" (*The True Bounds of Christian Freedom* [Edinburgh: Banner of Truth, 1978 reprint], pp. 144-45). As a believer you enjoy the privilege of a priest and the duty to offer spiritual sacrifices. Take a moment now to exercise your priestly office and offer God a spiritual sacrifice of praise for His grace extended to you.

2. In *Precious Remedies Against Satan's Devices* Thomas Brooks warned that Satan often confronts believers with the supposed impossibility of performing our spiritual duties. His advice: "Dwell more upon the necessity of the service and duty, than on the difficulty that doth attend the duty. . . . Though such-. . . services be hard and difficult, yet are they exceeding necessary for the honor of God, and the keeping up [of] his name in the world, and the keeping under of sin, and the strengthening of weak graces, and . . . stopping the mouths of unrighteous souls, who are ready to take all advantages to blaspheme the name of God, and throw dirt and contempt upon his people and ways" ([Edinburgh: Banner of Truth, 1987 reprint], pp. 117-18). Consider Brooks's advice the next time you are presented with the opportunity for spiritual sacrifice, but are tempted to turn away because of the apparent difficulty involved.

4

Security and Affection

Outline

Introduction
A. God's goodness in creation
B. God's goodness in mercy
C. God's goodness in redemption

Review
I. The Cornerstone of Our Privileges (v. 4)
II. The Kaleidoscope of Our Privileges (vv. 5-10)
   A. Union (v. 5*a*)
   B. Access (v. 5*b*)

Lesson
   C. Security (v. 6)
     1. A living stone
     2. An elect stone
     3. A precious stone
       a) It is irreplaceable
       b) It is important
       c) It is perfect
     4. A trustworthy stone
   D. Affection (vv. 7-8)
     1. Love for Christ
       a) A privilege of believers
       b) A test of faith
     2. Rejection of Christ
       a) Rejecting the appointed stone
       b) Stumbling over the appointed stone
       c) Being crushed by the appointed stone

Conclusion

Introduction

The story is told of a university student who had a rather lofty view of his own intellect. On one occasion he said to a pastor, "I have decided that I do not believe in God." "I see," the pastor replied. "Could you please describe for me the God you do not believe in?"

The student proceeded to sketch a caricature of God as unfair—as being anything but a God of goodness. After listening to that portrayal of God, the pastor wisely replied, "Well, we're in the same boat. I don't believe in that God either."

Most people, including many who call themselves Christians, have a warped view of God, viewing Him as less than good, kind, and benevolent. Their view of God is based on the common difficulties of life in a fallen world—the circumstances and conditions that plague our existence. But those who see beyond the physical realm recognize God's goodness and mercy. The God of the Bible is not an unkind, ungracious, unmerciful, overbearing deity. Christianity affirms the God of whom the psalmist said, "The goodness of God endureth continually" (Ps. 52:1, KJV*). In all aspects of life there is an overpowering sense of the goodness of God.

A. God's goodness in creation

> Those who truly experience the goodness of God are His children. Many choose to reject God and thereby reject His goodness, but we who by grace have come to God through Christ understand that He is good. God in Himself is an infinite and exhaustible treasure of all blessedness. His goodness is seen throughout creation—its vastness, beauty, variety, and intricacy of design. The immense variety of natural delights God has given and preserved in this fallen world shows how good He is. God could have created a drab world filled with plain people who all look alike and eat dirt! But God is good and has filled our days and hours with wondrous beauty.

* King James Version.

B. God's goodness in mercy

The goodness of God was demonstrated when man blighted God's created delights. He did not dispense unmixed wrath at once and rid earth of our kind. God even tempers His judgment of the ungodly with mercy. He allows the rain to fall on the just and the unjust. "Mercy triumphs over judgment" (James 2:13). God gives happiness to man, though man must suffer the sorrow that his sin produces.

C. God's goodness in redemption

Beyond the goodness demonstrated in creation and in His benevolence toward all mankind is God's goodness shown in the redemption of sinners. As Christians, we above all creation know His goodness.

In 1 Peter 2:4-10 we see God's goodness as expressed in the spiritual privileges of believers. Peter recounted eleven great privileges that are granted to believers by God's grace. We do not deserve them—they are gifts of grace from a good God, the Father of lights, from whom comes every good and perfect gift, and in whom there is no variableness or shifting shadow (James 1:17).

Review

I. THE CORNERSTONE OF OUR PRIVILEGES (v. 4; pp. 9-16)

II. THE KALEIDOSCOPE OF OUR PRIVILEGES (vv. 5-10)

A. Union (v. 5*a*; pp. 16-19)

B. Access (v. 5*b*; pp. 24-37, 42-50)

By giving us access through Christ, God has given us an open door into heaven. He has cried out for us to come into His presence and has given us admission to His presence at the throne of grace. The writer of Hebrews said, "Let us therefore draw near with confidence to the throne of grace" (4:16).

C. Security (v. 6)

"For this is contained in Scripture: 'Behold I lay in Zion a choice stone, a precious corner stone, and he who believes in Him shall not be disappointed.' "

As Peter turns the kaleidoscope once more, the beautiful colored stones of spiritual blessing are rearranged to show us our security in Christ. As believers, we have the conviction that we are secure in Jesus Christ forever. The key idea in verse 6 is that we will not be disappointed, ashamed, or disillusioned because the One in whom we have put our hope will not fail us.

Peter began his demonstration of the believer's security by pointing to Scripture: "This is contained in Scripture." Because Peter did not quote word for word, he did not use the formula "it is written," which is often used by New Testament writers to indicate a quotation from the Old Testament. It was not Peter's intent to specifically quote Scripture but to refer to the truth of its teaching regarding Christ.

1. A living stone

Peter's first reference to the Old Testament in affirming the security of the believer is from Isaiah 28:16, in which God says, "Behold, I am laying in Zion a stone, a tested stone, a costly cornerstone." According to Peter, the stone of Isaiah 28:16 is Christ.

First Peter 2:4 speaks of Christ as "a living stone." He is the foundation upon which we are built as living stones. He is also a living stone in that He has risen and is therefore alive.

The truth of Isaiah 28:16 regarding Christ is also affirmed by Paul in Romans 9:33. It was a very familiar and important Old Testament text (to the writers of the New Testament). It spoke of the Messiah—the coming Christ of God. It promised that when the Christ came, He would be the cornerstone of the new Temple of God.

At the beginning of Isaiah 28:16 is the word "behold." God was calling attention to the stone—He wanted undivided attention to be focused on it. Of that stone God said, "I am laying [it] in Zion." Zion here refers to Jerusalem, the city that occupies Mount Zion. Figuratively Mount Zion represents the New Covenant of grace, whereas Mount Sinai represents the Old Covenant of law (cf. Gal. 4:21-31).

2. An elect stone

First Peter 2:6 says that this stone is "a choice stone." That means it is elect—chosen by God. Both Isaiah's and Peter's analogy of stones would have set Jewish readers to thinking about the construction of the Temple in Jerusalem. First Kings 6:7 tells us that the Temple stones were prepared before they were brought to the site. They were shaped and cut at the stone quarry in accordance with a precise diagram of how the Temple was to be built. Each stone was then marked with a number so that it would be put into its proper place.

The Lord has used a similar process to build the New Covenant Temple (the church): all the stones (individuals) are elect—previously prepared for that destiny. They fit together according to a perfect pattern designed by the Spirit of God, who builds the Temple and places each stone according to its elect position.

3. A precious stone

   a) It is irreplaceable

   Not only is Christ an elect stone, but He is also "precious" (1 Pet. 2:6). The Greek word translated "precious" in this passage is translated "highly regarded" in Luke 7:2. It means "valuable," "costly," "without equal," or "irreplaceable." Christ is irreplaceable.

   b) It is important

   The most important stone in any building of Peter's time was the cornerstone. The Greek word *akrogōniaion* (translated "corner") literally means "at the extreme angle." A cornerstone established all the angles of the building. It set the direction of the walls both horizontally and vertically. All the angles of the building were kept in symmetry by the one cornerstone against which all other stones were compared.

c) It is perfect

To build the Temple we know as the church, it was necessary that the cornerstone be perfect. That perfect, elect, prepared cornerstone is none other than Jesus Christ. He is the stone that sets all the angles of God's spiritual Temple so that the church will be the perfect household of God. Just as the human builders of Peter's time tested their cornerstones, God has tested His and found Him perfect.

4. A trustworthy stone

Peter's final affirmation in verse 6 is that "he who believes in Him shall not be disappointed." Because of the perfection of God's chosen cornerstone, one of our great privileges as Christians is that we will never be disappointed when we trust in Christ.

We are rightfully confident in Christ because He is the perfect cornerstone who binds the church together. The Greek word translated "disappointed" carries the idea of having one's confidence misplaced or having one's hope in someone or something disappointed. But the Lord Jesus Christ will never let us down.

a) Isaiah 50:7—"The Lord God helps Me, therefore, I am not disgraced; therefore, I have set my face like flint, and I know that I shall not be ashamed." That is the confidence of one who believes in the true God.

b) Isaiah 54:1-10—" 'Shout for joy, O barren one, you who have borne no child; break forth into joyful shouting and cry aloud, you who have not travailed; for the sons of the desolate one will be more numerous than the sons of the married woman,' says the Lord. 'Enlarge the place of your tent; stretch out the curtains of your dwellings, spare not; lengthen your cords, and strengthen your pegs. For you will spread abroad to the right and to the left. And your descendants will possess nations, and they will resettle the desolate cities.

" 'Fear not, for you will not be put to shame; neither feel humiliated, for you will not be disgraced. . . . For your husband is your Maker, whose name is the Lord of hosts; and your Redeemer is the Holy One of Israel, who is called the God of all the earth. For the Lord has called you, like a wife forsaken and grieved in spirit, even like a wife of one's youth when she is rejected,' says your God. 'For a brief moment I forsook you, but with great compassion I will gather you. In an outburst of anger I hid my face from you for a moment; but with everlasting lovingkindness I will have compassion on you,' says the Lord your Redeemer. . . . 'My lovingkindness will not be removed from you.' "

c) Romans 8:28-39—"We know that God causes all things to work together for good to those who love God, to those who are called according to His purpose. For whom He foreknew, He also predestined to become conformed to the image of His Son, that He might be the first-born among many brethren; and whom He predestined, these He also called; and whom He called, these He also justified; and whom He justified, these He also glorified" (vv. 28-30). To those who doubted the glorification of believers, Paul said, "If God is for us, who is against us? . . . Who shall separate us from the love of Christ? . . . Neither death, nor life, nor angels, nor principalities, nor things present, nor things to come, nor powers, nor height, nor depth, nor any other created thing, shall be able to separate us from the love of God" (vv. 31-39).

d) Isaiah 28:16—"Behold, I am laying in Zion a stone, a tested stone, a costly cornerstone for the foundation, firmly placed. He who believes in it will not be disturbed." The Hebrew text literally reads, "He who believes in it will not be in a hurry." That means believers will not be in a hurry to run in fear because God has failed them. God promises that believers will have no reason to be confused, ashamed, or disappointed because the object of our trust, the Lord Jesus Christ, will never fail us.

D. Affection (vv. 7-8)

"This precious value, then, is for you who believe; but for those who disbelieve, 'The stone which the builders rejected, this became the very corner stone,' and, 'A stone of stumbling and a rock of offense'; for they stumble because they are disobedient to the word, and to this doom they were also appointed."

In verses 7-8 Peter again turns the kaleidoscope of our spiritual privileges, and we find ourselves viewing the marvelous privilege of having affection for our Lord.

1. Love for Christ

   a) A privilege of believers

   "This precious value"—the value of Christ as the cornerstone—belongs to those who believe. Indeed, "the love of God has been poured out within our hearts" (Rom. 5:5).

   First Peter 2:7 could be translated, "To you who believe He is precious." Christ is precious not only to God as His cornerstone, but He is also personally precious to believers. The disbelieving have no such affection for Christ. They reject Him, and He therefore becomes to them a stone of stumbling and a rock of offense. But to a believer, Christ is the most precious thing in life.

   b) A test of faith

   Affection for Christ is a bottom-line characteristic of true Christianity. It is where true Christian life begins. Every Christian is characterized by affection for Jesus Christ.

(1) John 8:42—Jesus said, "If God were your Father, you would love Me." A Christian is identified not by a past decision, but by a present love for Christ.

(2) John 14:15—"If you love Me, you will keep My commandments."

(3) John 14:21—"He who has My commandments and keeps them, he it is who loves Me; and he who loves Me shall be loved by My Father, and I will love him." Christianity is about loving Christ and obeying His commands.

(4) John 14:23-24—"If anyone loves Me, he will keep My word; and My Father will love him, and We will come to him, and make Our abode with him. He who does not love Me does not keep My words." Salvation, obedience, and love for Christ all go together.

(5) John 16:27—"The Father Himself loves you, because you have loved Me, and have believed." Believing in Christ and loving Him are inseparable.

(6) Matthew 10:37—"He who loves father or mother more than Me is not worthy of Me; and he who loves son or daughter more than Me is not worthy of Me." The saved have a surpassing and compelling love for Jesus Christ.

(7) 2 Corinthians 5:14—Paul said, "Christ's love compels us, because we are convinced that one died for all, and therefore all died" (NIV).

2. Rejection of Christ

   a) Rejecting the appointed stone

   After affirming the affection for Christ that exists in every believer, Peter then quoted the prediction of Psalm 118:22: "For those who disbelieve, 'The stone which the builders rejected, this became the very corner stone' " (1 Pet. 2:7). The world's assessment of

God's cornerstone was that He didn't measure up to their expectations, so they got rid of Him. The Greek word translated "rejected" means "to disallow after close examination." Christ was closely examined by the religious rulers of His day, but they rejected Him.

The Story with a Surprise Ending

The account of the rejection of Christ reads like a story with a surprise ending. The Jewish people were eagerly anticipating the kingdom of God. The rulers of Israel were waiting for the cornerstone of that kingdom to appear—the promised Messiah of God. Every Jewish mother hoped she would be the one to bear the Messiah. Four hundred years of silence followed the writing of Malachi, the last book of the Old Testament. During that time no prophet appeared in Israel, and the nation longed for some word from God. Then John the Baptist appeared and heralded the imminent approach of the Messiah. The nation was ecstatic.

Finally Jesus appeared and presented Himself as the cornerstone on which God would build His new Temple, the church. The religious leaders examined, scrutinized, and questioned Him. Like a literal stone, Jesus was picked up, turned over, and measured. But He didn't fit their building plans. They wanted a political, earthly deliverer. So they threw Him away—God's approved stone! The majority of Jewish people continue to do that today. The One so eagerly awaited for so long remains rejected.

The leaders of Israel thought Christ was worthless. But they were wrong. To God and to believers, Christ is precious. Peter affirms in verse 8 that those who believe in Him will never be disappointed. But recognizing the preciousness of Christ is an experience only for those who believe. Those who disbelieve view Him as a rejected stone—and their rejection was prophesied in Psalm 118:22. Yet the very stone they rejected became the cornerstone of God's building.

b) Stumbling over the appointed stone

Christ became not only the cornerstone, but also "a stone of stumbling and a rock of offense" (v. 8). Peter quoted from Isaiah 8:14-15, where Isaiah predicts that the Messiah would cause men and women to stumble and fall.

A "stone of stumbling" was a stone that caused someone to fall while walking along the road, while a "rock of offense" was a mass of rock like a cliff that could crush a man. The commentator R. C. H. Lenski adds, "Both terms reveal the destructiveness of Christ. . . . This stone is not one against which the disbelievers strike merely a foot and are thrown down and rise up more or less hurt, but one against which they strike with the entire body in a dreadful crash which knocks out their brains" (*The Interpretation of the Epistles of St. Peter, St. John and St. Jude* [Minneapolis: Augsburg, 1945], p. 96).

Thus the same stone approved by God as the cornerstone, which is precious to believers, is both a small stone (Gk., *lithos*) and large stone (Gk., *petra*) of devastation to unbelievers.

c) Being crushed by the appointed stone

Luke 20:18 says, "Everyone who falls on that stone will be broken to pieces; but on whomever it falls, it will scatter him like dust [lit. "grind him to powder"]." Peter tells us that men and women stumble over Christ "because they are disobedient to the word"—the gospel (1 Pet. 2:8). Unbelief and disobedience are terms closely associated with the unsaved, just as belief and obedience are closely associated with the saved.

To every individual Christ is either the cornerstone or the "rock of offense" (Gk., *petra skandalou*)—the rock against which men are crushed. He is a rock of judgment for unbelievers because they reject the gospel and refuse to obey it. First Peter 2:8 concludes, "To this doom they were also appointed." The unbeliever gets exactly what his choice demands—judgment. It is not the unbeliever's disobedience or unbelief that is appointed. The penalty for unbelief is what Peter refers to as "appointed."

63

Conclusion

Believers are privileged in having an affection for Christ. But ever since the time of Christ's appearing, there has been a vast number that reject Him. For those people He is an unacceptable stone, not fit as a cornerstone for the religious temple they want to build. So they throw Him aside and end up stumbling over Him, as He crushes them to powder in judgment. Their disobedience becomes their appointed destiny of doom. But by God's goodness and grace, Christ is not a stone of stumbling or rock of offense to believers. To them—to us—He is a precious cornerstone and beloved.

Focusing on the Facts

1. What is the key idea of 1 Peter 2:6 (see p. 56)?
2. Why did Peter use the phrase "this is contained in Scripture" to introduce his reference to the Old Testament (1 Pet. 2:6; see p. 56)?
3. To what does "Zion" refer in 1 Peter 2:6 (see p. 57)?
4. How does the building of Solomon's Temple illustrate the way in which God's New Testament temple—the church—is built (see p. 57)?
5. What are three reasons that Christ can be called "a precious cornerstone" (see pp. 57-58)?
6. What connotations does the word "disappointed" carry in 1 Peter 2:6 (see p. 58)?
7. What has God promised, according to Isaiah 28:16 (see pp. 59-60)?
8. What two kinds of people are contrasted in 1 Peter 2:7-8 (see p. 60)?
9. What is the most precious thing in the life of the believer (see p. 60)?
10. The saved have a _____ and _____ _____ for Jesus Christ (see p. 61).
11. What does the Greek word translated "rejected" in 1 Peter 2:7 mean (see p. 62)?
12. What was the surprise ending to the coming of Jesus Christ (see p. 62)?
13. For the unbeliever, God's cornerstone (Christ) is both a stone of _____ and a rock of _____ (see p. 62).

14. What two closely associated words describe the unsaved (see p. 63)?

15. Why is the unbeliever appointed to judgment _____
(1 Peter 2:8; see p. 63)?

Pondering the Principles

1. If you are a believer, you are a part of a spiritual building that is built on Jesus Christ, with measurements conforming to Him because He is the cornerstone. Thomas Watson wrote, "Our graces are imperfect, our comforts ebb and flow, but God's foundation standeth sure. They who are built upon this rock of God's eternal purpose, need not fear falling away; neither the power of man, not the violence of temptation, shall ever be able to overturn them" (*All Things for Good* [Edinburgh: Banner of Truth, 1986], p. 127). Take time now to praise God for His work in your life, both in bringing you to Him and preserving you for Him.

2. The eighteenth-century American theologian Jonathan Edwards wrote, "The greater the view and sense that one has of the infinite excellence and glory of God in Christ, and of how boundless is the length and breadth, depth and height of the love of Christ to sinners, the greater will be the astonishment one feels as he realizes how little he knows of such love to such a God, and to such a glorious Redeemer" (*Religious Affections* [Portland: Multnomah, 1984 abridged edition], p. 132). Christ's love for His people seems at times to inspire only a paltry return. However, the Puritan Thomas Brooks noted, "As a man rises higher and higher in his apprehensions of Christ, so he cannot but rise higher and higher in his affections to Christ. . . . The daily mercies and experiences that [he has] of the love of Christ, of the care of Christ, of the kindnesses and compassions of Christ working more and more towards [him], cannot but raise [his] affections more and more to him" (*Heaven on Earth* [Edinburgh: Banner of Truth, 1982 reprint], p. 243). What or who would people say is the great love of your life?

5
Election and Dominion

Outline

Introduction
A. The Cost of Being a Christian
B. The Privileges of Being a Christian

Review
 I. The Cornerstone of Our Privileges (v. 4)
II. The Kaleidoscope of Our Privileges (vv. 5-10)
A. Union (v. 5*a*)
B. Access (v. 5*b*)
C. Security (v. 6)
D. Affection (v. 7-8)

Lesson
E. Election (v. 9*a*)
1. The point of the passage
2. The Old Testament precedent
3. The New Testament parallel
4. The theological perspective
    a) Christians are chosen according to God's
          foreknowledge
    b) Christians are chosen the same way Jesus was
    c) Christians are chosen sovereignly by God
5. Some practical observations
    a) The doctrine of election crushes our pride
    b) The doctrine of election exalts God
    c) The doctrine of election promotes holiness
    d) The doctrine of election gives strength
    e) The doctrine of election produces joy

F. Dominion (v. 9b)
   1. The Old Testament precedent
   2. The New Testament parallel
      a) The office conferred
      b) The status attained

Conclusion

Introduction

A. The Cost of Being a Christian

The Bible says much about the cost of being a Christian. Many times our Lord emphasized the cost of discipleship. In Luke 14:26-31 He says to the multitudes, "If anyone comes to Me, and does not hate his own father and mother and wife and children and brothers and sisters, yes, and even his own life, he cannot be My disciple. Whoever does not carry his own cross and come after Me cannot be My disciple. For which one of you, when he wants to build a tower, does not first sit down and calculate the cost, to see if he has enough to complete it? Otherwise, when he has laid a foundation, and is not able to finish, all who observe it begin to ridicule him, saying, 'This man began to build and was not able to finish.' Or what king, when he sets out to meet another king in battle, will not first sit down and take counsel whether he is strong enough with ten thousand men to encounter the one coming against him with twenty thousand?"

In Matthew 10:37-38 Jesus says, "He who loves father or mother more than Me is not worthy of Me; and he who loves son or daughter more than Me is not worthy of Me. And he who does not take up his cross and follow after Me is not worthy of Me."

There is a cost of being a Christian, and that cost must be assessed. Those who come to a true knowledge of Christ also come to understand that certain sacrifices are necessary in the Christian life. We must do certain things and turn away from other things. That is a continuing emphasis throughout the New Testament.

B. The Privileges of Being a Christian

In contrast to that theme is what we find in 1 Peter 2:4-10: the dividends of being a Christian. Peter deals here with the rewards, treasures, and riches that believers receive. He does not deal with what we have had to give up but with the spiritual privileges that belong to every believer in Jesus Christ. Throughout the New Testament there is great emphasis on our spiritual privileges.

1. Romans 9:22-23—"What if God, although willing to demonstrate His wrath and to make His power known, endured with much patience vessels of wrath prepared for destruction? . . . He did so in order that He might make known the riches of His glory upon vessels of mercy, which He prepared beforehand for glory." We who are Christians are the vessels of mercy upon whom the riches of God's glory are and will be poured.

2. Romans 11:33—"Oh, the depth of the riches both of the wisdom and knowledge of God!"

3. Ephesians 1:7-8—"In [Christ] we have redemption through His blood, [and] the forgiveness of our trespasses, according to the riches of His grace, which He lavished upon us"—not *will* lavish but has lavished already.

4. Ephesians 2:7—God will show "the surpassing riches of His grace in kindness toward us in Christ Jesus."

5. Ephesians 3:8—Paul's main ministry was "to preach to the Gentiles the unfathomable riches of Christ."

6. Ephesians 3:16—Paul prayed for God to strengthen the church "according to the riches of His glory."

7. Philippians 4:19—"God shall supply all your needs according to His riches in glory in Christ Jesus."

All who are Christians should be filled with joy and thanksgiving in contemplating those great truths!

Review

I. THE CORNERSTONE OF OUR PRIVILEGES (v. 4; pp. 9-16)

II. THE KALEIDOSCOPE OF OUR PRIVILEGES (vv. 5-10)

A. Union (v. 5a; pp. 16-19)

B. Access (v. 5b; pp. 24-37, 42-50)

C. Security (v. 6; pp. 56-60)

D. Affection (v. 7-8; pp. 60-64)

God has granted believers the exclusive privilege of loving Christ. The apostle Paul said, "Grace be with all those who love our Lord Jesus Christ with a love incorruptible" (Eph. 6:24). There is no more exhilarating emotion than the joy of love.

On the other hand, unbelievers are doomed by their disobedience, unbelief, and lack of love for Christ. Those three attitudes prove that they are unregenerate. Paul also said, "If anyone does not love the Lord, let him be accursed" (1 Cor. 16:22).

Lesson

E. Election (v. 9a)

"You are a chosen race."

1. The point of the passage

With another turn of the kaleidoscope of our spiritual privileges, Peter now focuses on the doctrine of election. Peter ties verse 9 to verse 8 with an emphatic adversative—a strong "but" that contrasts those to whom he had been referring with those he was about to address. The idea is, "Unlike those who are destined for destruction because of their unbelief, you on the other hand are a chosen race." The Greek term translated "race" refers to the source of a particular group of people. Peter emphasized that Christians are a race produced from a divine source.

2. The Old Testament precedent

Throughout 1 Peter 2:4-10 Peter makes extensive use of the Old Testament. He alludes to it in verses 4-5 and makes direct quotations in verses 6-8. In verse 9 Peter alludes to Deuteronomy 7:6-9: "You are a holy people to the Lord your God; the Lord your God has chosen you to be a people for His own possession out of all the peoples who are on the face of the earth. The Lord did not set His love on you nor choose you because you were more in number than any of the peoples, for you were the fewest of all peoples, but because the Lord loved you and kept the oath which He swore to your forefathers, the Lord brought you out by a mighty hand, and redeemed you from the house of slavery, from the hand of Pharaoh king of Egypt. Know therefore that the Lord your God, He is God." Peter viewed the church as the redeemed community of God, chosen just as Israel was chosen.

In Isaiah 43:21 we find a similar affirmation regarding Israel: "The people whom I formed for Myself, will declare My praise." God identified Israel as His chosen people, a designation they have retained throughout the centuries.

3. The New Testament parallel

First Peter 2:9 tells us there is another chosen race: the church. First Peter 1:1-2 explains that the church was "chosen according to the foreknowledge of God the Father, by the sanctifying work of the Spirit."

God's choice of believers is our most important privilege because all the other privileges come as a result of His choice. If you are a Christian, you should celebrate the privilege of being chosen by God. Scripture repeatedly affirms the great truth of election.

a) John 15:16—Jesus said to His disciples, "You did not choose Me, but I chose you."

b) Acts 13:48—"When the Gentiles heard [that the gospel applied to them], they began rejoicing and glorifying the word of the Lord; and as many as had been appointed to eternal life believed." God appointed them to eternal life, and they believed.

c) Romans 9:13-16—Defending God's choice in election, Paul cited Old Testament precedent: "It is written, 'Jacob I loved, but Esau I hated.' What shall we say then? There is no injustice with God, is there? May it never be! For He says to Moses, 'I will have mercy on whom I have mercy, and I will have compassion on whom I have compassion.' So then it does not depend on the man who wills or the man who runs, but on God who has mercy."

d) Romans 11:5—"There has also come to be at the present time a remnant [of believing Israelites] according to God's gracious choice."

e) 1 Corinthians 1:9—"God is faithful, through whom you were called into fellowship with His Son."

f) Ephesians 1:3-5—"Blessed be the God and Father of our Lord Jesus Christ, who has blessed us with every spiritual blessing in the heavenly places in Christ, just as He chose us in Him before the foundation of the world. . . . He predestined us to adoption as sons through Jesus Christ to Himself."

g) 1 Thessalonians 1:4—Paul encouraged the Thessalonian church by pointing out the fact of their election: "Knowing, brethren beloved by God, His choice of you."

h) 2 Thessalonians 2:13—Likewise he said, "We should always give thanks to God for you, brethren beloved by the Lord, because God has chosen you from the beginning for salvation."

i) 2 Timothy 1:9—God "saved us, and called us with a holy calling, not according to our works, but according to His own purpose and grace which was granted us in Christ Jesus from all eternity."

j) 2 Timothy 2:10—Paul said, "I endure all things for the sake of those who are chosen, that they also may obtain the salvation which is in Christ Jesus."

k) Revelation 13:8—"All who dwell on the earth will worship [the Beast], everyone whose name has not been written from the foundation of the world in the book of life of the Lamb who has been slain." The names of God's chosen were written in the Lamb's Book of Life before the foundation of the world (cf. Rev. 17:8).

l) Revelation 20:15—"If anyone's name was not found written in the book of life, he was thrown into the lake of fire."

4. The theological perspective

   a) Christians are chosen according to God's foreknowledge

   God did not choose anyone because of what he or she did or will do. He sovereignly determined to set His love upon us for divine reasons that we may never fully understand. When Peter stated that God chose us according to His foreknowledge (1 Pet. 1:2), he did not mean that God knew beforehand what we were going to do and chose us based on that knowledge. Foreknowledge is a theological reference to God's deliberate choice.

   b) Christians are chosen the same way Jesus was

   A good example of what Peter meant by God's choice is in 1 Peter 2:6, which refers to Christ as a "choice stone." Believers are chosen and predestined in the same way that Christ was chosen by God to fulfill a holy purpose. God said of Christ, "Behold, My Servant, whom I uphold; My chosen one in whom My soul delights" (Isa. 42:1).

God certainly didn't look down the corridors of history and say to Himself, "Oh, I see, a man named Jesus will do great things, so I'll choose Him." Christ was chosen by the absolute sovereignty of God, and believers are chosen in the same way.

c) Christians are chosen sovereignly by God

If God's decisions were based on man's actions, then man would be sovereign and would deserve the credit for his own faith. That assumes man can and does seek God. Salvation would thus be a human work with God relegated to the status of a second-class deity who doesn't deserve as much glory as those who seek Him. What a horrid contrast to what Scripture teaches! The Bible affirms that God is sovereign, that man gets no credit for his own believing, and that man cannot and does not seek God. God is never portrayed as a victim of man's choices; instead, He is sovereign, and believers are chosen.

5. Some practical observations

Jeremiah was chosen before he was even born (Jer. 1:5). In the same way, believers were chosen by God before the foundation of the world. That choice is activated in time when the Spirit of God prompts the hearts of the individuals concerned to believe.

a) The doctrine of election crushes our pride

That God sovereignly chooses men and women for salvation devastates our pride. Yet it affirms that man is totally dependent on God to respond in faith toward Him (Eph. 2:8-9).

b) The doctrine of election exalts God

Election affirms that salvation is all of God. That exalts God more than any other doctrine in Scripture.

74

c) The doctrine of election promotes holiness

Christians ought to be so grateful to God for His grace that they will live for Him at any price—consumed with a passion for obedience.

d) The doctrine of election gives strength

When God chooses, that choice is eternal and unequivocal. We have nothing to fear and have every right to be confident and strong in faith.

e) The doctrine of election produces joy

God's sovereign choice is the only hope for wretched sinners. Nothing could bring more joy because it produces such profound gratitude.

F. Dominion (v. 9*b*)

"You are . . . a royal priesthood."

Believers are a royal priesthood—another privilege with an Old Testament parallel. Not only are we priests (already discussed in v. 5—see pp. 24-37, 42-50), but we are also part of a royal household. That is a new concept because in the Old Testament the offices of king and priest were kept separate (with one striking exception, Melchizedek, whom we will soon discuss).

1. The Old Testament precedent

Peter's idea of a royal priesthood is drawn from Exodus 19:6, where God said of Israel, "You shall be to Me a kingdom of priests." However Israel forfeited the privilege offered to them. Israel was not able to realize dominion because they apostatized and executed their Messiah. Peter affirms that at present the church is the royal priesthood of God.

2. The New Testament parallel

   a) The office conferred

   The royal priesthood of the church serves the Lord Jesus Christ, who is the King of kings and Lord of lords. Beyond that, it exercises dominion and rule. We not only serve the King, but we also reign with Him.

   b) The status attained

   The Greek word translated "royal" in 1 Peter 2:9 (*basileios*) can refer to a royal palace, sovereignty, crown, or monarchy. Here the idea is royalty in general. Thus the spiritual house in verse 5 refers to a royal house— not a building but a sphere of dominion, such as the royal house of England or France. Peter described the church as a royal house of priests. That squares with other New Testament revelation.

   (1) Revelation 1:6—Christ "has made us to be a kingdom [of] priests."

   (2) Revelation 5:10—It is said of God and the church, "Thou hast made them to be a kingdom and priests to our God; and they will reign upon the earth."

   (3) Revelation 20:6—"Blessed and holy is the one who has a part in the first resurrection; over these the second death has no power, but they will be priests of God and of Christ and will reign with Him."

   (4) Hebrews 7:14-17—The only person who could have established a royal house of priests is the Lord Jesus Christ. Only He was both a king and a priest: "It is evident that our Lord was descended from Judah, a tribe with reference to which Moses spoke nothing concerning priests. And this is clearer still, if another priest arises according to the likeness of Melchizedek, who has become such not on the basis of a law of physical require-

ment, but according to the power of an indestructible life. For it is witnessed of Him, 'Thou art a priest forever according to the order of Melchizedek.' "

Melchizedek was unique. He was the only royal priest in the Old Testament. Christ was a royal priest similar to Melchizedek in that He didn't inherit His priesthood by coming through the priestly line (Levi). Rather, He came through the royal line of Judah. Christ is King, and those who believe in Him will reign with Him.

(5) 1 Corinthians 6:1-3—Paul said, "Does any one of you, when he has a case against his neighbor, dare to go to law before the unrighteous, and not before the saints? Or do you not know that the saints will judge the world? And if the world is judged by you, are you not competent to constitute the smallest law courts? Do you not know that we shall judge angels? How much more, matters of this life?"

If you are a Christian, your future is that of a royal priest. You will spend eternity giving offerings to the Lord God and reigning with Christ. You will have dominion over whatever dimensions of heavenly existence God assigns to you, and you will rule over angels. Because there is no one between you and the Lord, you are a priest. Because there is no one over you but the Lord, you are a king. Those are privileges far beyond those of the Old Testament priesthood.

Conclusion

The many privileges God has given believers should make us grateful to God for all He has done. That gratitude should be expressed both in thanksgiving and confession. If we are grateful for the spiritual privileges that have been freely given us, we will lift our hearts in thankful praise to God and confess our sins, which so often stem from ingratitude.

Focusing on the Facts

1. What doctrine is emphasized in 1 Peter 2:9 (see p. 70)?
2. To which two passages in the Old Testament does 1 Peter 2:9 allude? How do they relate to Peter's subject (see p. 71)?
3. Why is election our most important spiritual privilege (see p. 71)?
4. According to Romans 9, what does God's choice of the saved depend on (see p. 72)?
5. Believers are chosen the same way _____ was (see pp. 73-74).
6. For God's choice to depend on what man does, what would we have to assume about man? What does the Bible say about that (see p. 74)?
7. What effect does the sovereign choice of God have on man's pride (see p. 74)?
8. What is new about the idea of a royal priesthood (see p. 75)?
9. We not only serve the King, we also _____ with Him (see p. 76).
10. What does the future hold for Christians (1 Cor. 6:1-3; see p. 77)?

Pondering the Principles

1. Of the great reformers of the eighteenth century—Whitefield, Wesley, Rowlands, Venn, Toplady, and others—it was said, "They knew nothing of the modern notion that Christ is in every man, and that all possess something good within, which they have only to stir up and use in order to be saved. They never flattered men and women in this fashion. They told them plainly that they were dead, and must be made alive again; that they were guilty, lost, helpless, and hopeless, and in imminent danger of eternal ruin. Strange and paradoxical as it may seem to some, their first step towards making men good was to show them that they were utterly bad; and their primary argument in persuading men to do something for their souls was to convince them that they could do nothing at all" (J. C. Ryle, *Christian Leaders of the 18th Century* [Edinburgh: Banner of Truth, 1978 reprint], pp. 26-27). While the doctrines of man's total depravity and God's sovereign election humble man's pride, they produce a profound gratitude in those who realize the extent of

God's mercy extended by grace. What has the spiritual privilege of being chosen by God meant in your life?

2. Paul instructed Timothy to "set an example for the believers in speech, in life, in love, in faith and in purity" (1 Tim. 4:12, NIV). That is particularly appropriate advice for someone who has the privilege of being a royal priest and will therefore be closely scrutinized by others. If you are a Christian, you are a royal priest and an example of Christ for anyone you come in contact with. Read Philippians 2:5-8. How do others think and behave based on your example of Christ? Let that motivate you as you check for any necessary changes in your life-style and habits.

6

Separation, Possession, Illumination, Compassion, and Proclamation

Outline

Introduction

Review
I. The Cornerstone of Our Privileges (v. 4)
II. The Kaleidoscope of Our Privileges (vv. 5-10)
   A. Union (v. 5a)
   B. Access (v. 5b)
   C. Security (v. 6)
   D. Affection (v. 7-8)
   E. Election (v. 9a)
   F. Dominion (v. 9b)

Lesson
   G. Separation (v. 9c)
     1. The message of holiness
       a) The Old Testament precedent
         (1) The calling of Israel
         (2) The failure of Israel
       b) The New Testament parallel
     2. The meaning of holiness
     3. The means of holiness
     4. The progress of holiness
       a) Sanctification is progressive
         (1) The explanation
         (2) The exhortations

Introduction

Peter wrote 1 Peter to scattered Christians who were experiencing difficult circumstances. They were paying the price of living out their Christian lives in a hostile world. First Peter 2:4-10 contains the heart of the encouragement we find in Peter's first epistle. It is a description of the spiritual privileges God has given all believers by His grace.

In this passage Peter takes the simple truths of salvation and rotates them as you would rotate the end of a kaleidoscope. Those simple and magnificent truths are transformed into patterns beautiful beyond description. Each time we observe a turn of Peter's kaleidoscope, we see another arrangement of the marvelous privileges that are ours in Christ. This passage is not about duty; it's all about privilege.

Review

I. THE CORNERSTONE OF OUR PRIVILEGES (v. 4; pp. 9-16)

II. THE KALEIDOSCOPE OF OUR PRIVILEGES (vv. 5-10)

    A. Union (v. 5*a*; pp. 16-19)

    B. Access (v. 5*b*; pp. 24-37, 42-50)

    C. Security (v. 6; pp. 56-60)

    D. Affection (vv. 7-8; pp. 60-64)

    E. Election (v. 9*a*; pp. 70-75)

    F. Dominion (v. 9*b*; pp. 75-77)

Lesson

    G. Separation (v. 9*c*)

"You are . . . a holy nation."

Christians are a "nation" (Gk., *ethnos,* from which we get the word *ethnic*). More than that, we are a "holy nation." That means we are a people separated or set apart.

    1. The message of holiness

        a) The Old Testament precedent

            (1) The calling of Israel

            We find quotations and allusions to the Old Testament throughout 1 Peter 2:4-10. By describing the church as "a holy nation," Peter was drawing on God's description of Israel in Exodus 19:6: "You shall be to Me a kingdom of priests and a holy nation." Similar descriptions of God's people are found in Leviticus 19:2; 20:26; Deuteronomy 7:6; and Isaiah 62:12.

(2) The failure of Israel

But Israel's history was tragic. By unbelief the nation forfeited the great privilege of belonging uniquely to God.

b) The New Testament parallel

The tragedy of Israel's apostasy became a blessing for the Gentiles according to Romans 11:7-12. God now has a new unique people—the church, consisting of both Jew and Gentile (Eph. 2:11-12). The church will remain God's unique people until the nation of Israel as a whole turns in faith to the Messiah.

2. The meaning of holiness

Holiness means that we have been set apart unto God. Although that includes being set apart for service, the primary emphasis is our relationship with God. In salvation God does the inconceivable: He draws wicked, vile sinners to Himself. He takes them out of darkness into light, out of death into life, out of the kingdom of Satan into the kingdom of His dear Son (Col. 1:13), and out of communion with Satan and demons into communion with Himself. The theological word often used to describe that is sanctification. As a holy nation, we are separated from what is unholy and are devoted to God.

3. The means of holiness

We were made holy by means of God's choice. First Peter 1:1-2 says we "are chosen according to the foreknowledge of God the Father, by the sanctifying work of the Spirit, that [we] may obey Jesus Christ and be [in a covenant relationship with Him by being] sprinkled with His blood."

Salvation is the work of God by which we are set apart. We are set apart not just *from* sin and hell, but *to* an intimate relationship with God. That new relationship is manifested by obedience to God produced by the Holy Spirit. Therefore we are "born again to a living hope" by the Word, which the Spirit applies to our hearts in salvation (1 Pet. 1:3).

a) Acts 15:7-9—Peter said to the apostles and elders, "Brethren, you know that in the early days God made a choice among you, that by my mouth the Gentiles should hear the word of the gospel and believe. And God, who knows the heart, bore witness to them [the Gentiles], giving them the Holy Spirit, just as He also did to us; and He made no distinction between us and them, cleansing their hearts by faith." That is a picture of what it means to be sanctified—the believer is holy, cleansed of sin, set apart from sin, and set apart unto God.

b) Hebrews 10:10—"By this [God's will] we have been sanctified through the offering of the body of Jesus Christ once for all." Sanctification goes hand-in-hand with salvation.

c) Hebrews 10:14-15—"By one offering [Christ on the cross] He has perfected for all time those who are sanctified. And the Holy Spirit also bears witness to us." Sanctification is bound up in salvation. You became part of the holy nation by the Spirit's work of salvation in you.

d) 1 Corinthians 1:30—"By [God's] doing you are in Christ Jesus, who became to us wisdom from God, and righteousness and sanctification, and redemption."

4. The progress of holiness

a) Sanctification is progressive

(1) The explanation

Sanctification is more than just a state of being. It is a progressive pattern of life. When the Holy Spirit set us apart unto God, we became His special possession. That doesn't mean we will never

85

sin again, but it does mean we are no longer in bondage to sin, the devil, and death. That's positional sanctification.

Beyond positional sanctification lies progressive sanctification—the change that occurs in our pattern of life through the power of the Spirit. When the Spirit of God sets us apart unto God, we begin to live for God. We begin a process of being progressively separated from the sin that once dominated us. That's why 1 Peter 1:2 says we have been sanctified and why 1 Peter 1:15-16 says we are to be sanctified.

Sanctification involves both positional and progressive aspects. Positional sanctification means that we were taken out of the kingdom of darkness and placed into the kingdom of God's dear Son. It can no longer be said that the devil is our father (cf. Luke 8:41). Rather, our Father is God Himself. We belong to Him and are separated from the penalty of sin.

The progressive reality of sanctification is that our lives are more and more conformed to God's holiness. Our lives demonstrate the reality of our position. We could say that we are becoming what we already are in Christ.

(2) The exhortations

  (a) 1 Thessalonians 4:3—"This is the will of God, your sanctification; that is, that you abstain from sexual immorality." Paul was alluding to progressive sanctification here. Of the three kinds of sanctification—positional, progressive, and ultimate—only in ultimate sanctification do we become completely like Christ. In the life to come we will be totally set apart to Him. At salvation we are given the privilege of being set apart unto God to be His possession.

  (b) Romans 6:6—"Our old self was crucified with Him, that our body of sin might be done away with, that we should no longer be slaves to sin." Because we are no longer in uncontrollable bondage to sin, we need to stop living as if we were.

(c) Acts 20:32—Paul said, "I commend you to God and to the word of His grace, which is able to build you up and to give you the inheritance among all those who are sanctified." The eternal inheritance Paul spoke of belongs to all who are saved, and all who are saved are also sanctified.

(d) Acts 26:17-18—The Lord said to Paul, "I am sending you, to open their [the Gentiles'] eyes so that they may turn from darkness to light and from the dominion of Satan to God, in order that they may receive forgiveness of sins and an inheritance among those who have been sanctified by faith in Me." Here we see a close connection between sanctification and salvation. By faith we are sanctified, saved, and forgiven. By faith we also receive an inheritance, move from darkness to light, and turn from the dominion of Satan to God.

We have the wonderful privilege of being a holy people. We've been set apart to God and are no longer owned by Satan. We are no longer slaves in bondage to sin because we have entered into a new relationship. We work toward living in the light of that holy identity—progressively living up to our position. Sin creates disaster in our lives because it is so contrary to our union with Christ. It defies everything about our character as a holy people set apart unto God.

b) Sanctification is practical

(1) What it is not

(a) The separation of a monk

Practical sanctification does not require that we isolate ourselves from the world. That

87

would take care of our outer circumstances, but would not affect the corruption that resides in our hearts. Externalism will not transform anyone's life.

(b) The separation of a Pharisee

The Pharisees also attempted to achieve holiness through external means. But they only whitewashed what was on the inside—the spiritual equivalent of dead men's bones (Matt. 23:27). A Pharisee painted the outside but remained wretched on the inside. He circumspectly observed legalistic practices, but there was no inward transformation.

(c) The separation of a Stoic

Sanctification is not achieved by the Stoic, who believes it is a sin to be happy. Walking around with a dour look on one's face as if that indicates a serious mind is a pious reaction that is wholly external. It will not transform one's inner life.

(2) What it is

Practical sanctification involves cultivating personal intimacy with Christ. We are a people set apart unto Christ both positionally and personally. All Christians are on intimate terms with their Savior.

James 4:8 says, "Draw near to God and He will draw near to you." A sanctified heart will cultivate an intimate relationship with Jesus Christ. First Corinthians 6:17 says, "The one who joins himself to the Lord is one spirit with Him." Because we have been joined to Christ, immorality is a particularly vile thing for Christians. We actually join Christ to our immoral acts (1 Cor. 6:15-16).

As part of a holy nation, we are both positionally and intimately set apart to Christ. Holiness will be evident in our lives only when we know Christ intimately. However, many are trying to live the Christian life apart from the living Christ, depending on quasi-Christian psychology. Introspection, improvement in one's self-image, and self-analysis are no substitute for intimacy with Christ, which is what compels us toward holiness.

H. Possession (v. 9*d*)

"You are . . . a people for God's own possession."

That reflects Exodus 19:5: "If you will indeed obey My voice and keep My covenant, then you shall be My own possession among all the peoples." Peter might also have been thinking about Isaiah 43:21: "The people whom I formed for Myself, will declare My praise" (cf. Deut. 7:6; 14:2; 26:18; Mal. 3:17).

The Greek word translated "possession" means "to acquire," "purchase," or "acquire for a price." We find it in Ephesians 1:14, which speaks of "the redemption of God's own possession." We are God's own possession because He paid the price for us.

1. Acts 20:28—"The church . . . [was] purchased with [Christ's] own blood."

2. 1 Corinthians 6:20—"You have been bought with a price." That price was the death of the Lord Jesus Christ.

3. Titus 2:14—Christ "gave Himself for us, that He might redeem [or purchase] us from every lawless deed and purify for Himself a people for His own possession." God by sovereign election chose us and by the sacrifice of Christ paid the price to buy us back. Therefore we are God's personal possessions.

Jesus said, "I am the good shepherd; and I know My own, and My own know Me" (John 10:14). I remember sitting in seminary chapel and singing one of my favorite hymns, "I Am His and He Is Mine" by nineteenth-century lyricist Wade Robinson. From the early days of my seminary education, I acquired a special love for the truth that I belong to

Christ. As Christians we enjoy the privilege of belonging wholly to God.

I. Illumination (v. 9e)

"That you may proclaim the excellencies of Him who has called you out of darkness into His marvelous light."

1. The meaning of darkness

The darkness from which we have been called is the disastrous state of sin. That state is the darkness of Satan, who is the prince of darkness (cf. John 14:30; Eph. 6:12). The darkness consists primarily of two things: ignorance and immorality. The unregenerate are in a state of intellectual darkness that prevents their seeing the truth. And they are in moral darkness which prevents their knowing and acting on what is right.

2. The means of deliverance

a) The call of God

But Peter affirms that the regenerate—Christians— have been called out of darkness. The word translated "called" refers to the saving initiative of God. In the New Testament epistles it does not refer to God's general call to the masses of humanity but to the effectual call of God that always ends in salvation.

b) The transformation of a believer

It is our privilege to have been called out of darkness into the light. Where once we were in intellectual and moral darkness, now we understand the truth and have the ability to do right. We have a true knowledge of God, and we obey Him.

Those two qualities are absent in the lives of the unregenerate. In salvation we were rescued from ignorance of God's will and the inability to perform it. That transition can be easily forgotten. The longer we are Christians, the harder it becomes to remember what we were like before we knew Christ.

How Deep Is the Darkness!

Satan's darkness is so pervasive that the unregenerate can be described as people in darkness and people of darkness. They actually love the darkness. John 3:19 says, "This is the judgment, that the light is come into the world, and men loved the darkness rather than the light; for their deeds were evil." No one can come to a knowledge of God's light by himself. A person can be an atheist and never give serious thought to the light of God because darkness does not comprehend the light (John 1:5). The depth of spiritual darkness is profound. We depend completely on God to call us out of that darkness.

J. Compassion (v. 10)

"You once were not a people, but now you are the people of God; you had not received mercy, but now you have received mercy."

The book of Hosea tells us that the prophet's adulterous wife "gave birth to a daughter. And the Lord said to him, 'Name her Lo-ruhamah, for I will no longer have compassion on the house of Israel, that I should ever forgive them. But I will have compassion on the house of Judah and deliver them by the Lord their God, and will not deliver them by bow, sword, battle, horses, or horsemen.' When she had weaned Lo-ruhamah, she conceived and gave birth to a son. And the Lord said, 'Name him Lo-ammi, for you are not My people and I am not Your God. Yet the number of the sons of Israel will be like the sand of the sea, which cannot be measured or numbered; and it will come about that, in the place where it is said to them, "You are not My people," it will be said to them, "You are the sons of the living God" ' " (1:6-10).

1. The people of God's mercy

Peter applied an Old Testament description of Israel to the New Testament church. Paul did the same thing in Romans 9:25-26: "I will call those who were not My people, 'My people,' and her who was not beloved, 'Beloved.' And it shall be that in the place where it was said to them, 'You are not My people,' there they shall be called sons of the living God" (cf. Hos. 2:23; 1:10). Peter and Paul referred to the church as those "who were once not a people, but now are the people of God" (1 Pet. 2:10; Rom. 9:25-26). That is particularly true of Gentiles in the church.

When God said we were not His people but would become His people, He meant that He was going to extend His mercy to us. According to 1 Peter 2:10, we were once not God's people because we had not received God's mercy. God's mercy is His compassion for His people. That is why we can say that we enjoy the spiritual privilege of compassion from our Lord.

2. The meaning of God's mercy

Mercy is the same thing as compassion. The concept is sometimes translated "lovingkindness" in the Old Testament. Because of God's compassion, He withholds the just punishment of our sin.

a) General mercy

There are two kinds of mercy exercised by God. One is general mercy. That is seen in God's working in the creative order, such as God's providential care for all mankind. God's patience and pity benefit all sinners, even though God has every right to destroy those who don't know Him.

(1) Lamentations 3:22—"The Lord's lovingkindnesses indeed never cease, for His compassions never fail." Everyone benefits from the Lord's compassion.

(2) Psalm 145:9—"The Lord is good to all, and His mercies are over all His works." It is because of God's mercy that people aren't immediately consumed by God's wrath.

b) Special mercy

   (1) A special effect

      However, 1 Peter 2:10 speaks not about general mercy, but about the special mercy of God extended to the elect. It is a unique mercy and is totally undeserved by those who enjoy it. For some people God is generally merciful—He alleviates the present full potential for judgment caused by the disaster of sin, but only in this life. For others— those who are elect—God alleviates that judgment forever. They receive not only general mercy in this life but also special mercy in the life to come. God bestows His special compassion on the elect by forgiving their sin, whereas in the case of the unregenerate He simply withholds judgment until the future.

   (2) A special choice

      God chooses to extend His special compassion because it is His pleasure to do so. Because He is a God of love, He chose to love the elect.

      (*a*) Micah 7:18—"Who is a God like Thee, who pardons iniquity and passes over the rebellious act of the remnant of His possession?"

      (*b*) Romans 9:15, 20—God said, "I will have mercy on whom I have mercy, and I will have compassion on whom I have compassion. . . . The thing molded will not say to the molder, 'Why did you make me like this,' will it?"

   (3) A special reason

      It is not the wretchedness of the sinner that causes God to show mercy. God does not show compassion because He feels sorry for sinners or is emotionally distraught over their predicament. If that was what caused God to extend His mercy, He would be obligated to extend mercy to all.

It is not because some sinners are more worthy of mercy than others that God extends His mercy. If that were the reason for God's compassion, He wouldn't be extending mercy; He would be meeting an obligation. But God's mercy means that He is withholding the just punishment that all men deserve.

God is not merciful to some because Christ made it possible for Him to be merciful. We were chosen by His sovereign love before the world began. Theologian A. W. Pink observed that mercy arises solely from God's imperial pleasure (*The Doctrines of Election and Justification* [Grand Rapids: Baker, 1974], cf. p. 55). God showed mercy to us simply because He chose to do so. That should escalate your sense of being a privileged person!

(*a*) Psalm 57:10—"Thy mercy is great unto the heavens" (KJV).

(*b*) Psalm 103:11—"Great is his mercy toward them that fear him" (KJV). It is God's mercy that saves us and grants us an eternal inheritance.

(*c*) 2 Corinthians 1:3—"Blessed be the God and Father of our Lord Jesus Christ, the Father of mercies and God of all comfort."

(*d*) Titus 3:5—"[God] saved us, not on the basis of deeds which we have done in righteousness, but according to His mercy."

(*e*) Psalm 136:1—"O give thanks unto the Lord; for he is good: for his mercy endureth forever" (KJV).

(*f*) Psalm 59:16—"I will sing aloud of [God's] mercy in the morning" (KJV).

K. Proclamation (v. 9*e*)

"That you may proclaim the excellencies of Him who has called you out of darkness into His marvelous light."

Although this privilege brings us back to verse 9, conceptually it must be addressed last because it explains the purpose of all our privileges in Christ: "that [we] may proclaim the excellencies of Him." Christians enjoy the high privilege of being ambassadors of the living God.

1. The meaning of proclamation

The Greek word translated "proclaim" is used only here in the New Testament. It is an unusual word meaning "to advertise" or "to publish." It meant that something was to be told that would otherwise be unknown. "Excellencies" speak of the ability to do heroic deeds. So Christians have the privilege of telling what the world would otherwise not know concerning God's heroic deeds.

2. The purpose of proclamation

God has the ability to do mighty and powerful acts. Peter was not referring to excellencies as attributes or intrinsic qualities, but as powerful and heroic deeds.

It would be an honor to be chosen to be an ambassador of the United States. In that role, we could represent this nation's power and abilities. But we have been chosen to be ambassadors of the living God, who is able to do heroic deeds on a miraculous scale. When you have an opportunity to speak about who you represent, you can say, "I have the privilege of announcing the mighty and heroic deeds of the living God who has called me into His service."

According to Paul, we are ambassadors for Christ (2 Cor. 5:20). We have been given the Holy Spirit and now are witnesses for God. What a great privilege!

Conclusion

The reason we have all those glorious privileges is that we are in Christ. We are in union with God because we are in Christ, and Christ is one with God. We have access to the Father's glorious presence because we have access through Christ. We are secure in our relationship to God because we are in Christ and He is secure in His relationship to God—He is part of the triune Godhead. We have affection for our Lord, and we love Him because He first loved us. We have been chosen in Him before the foundation of the world. We have dominion because we reign with Him. We are a separate, holy nation because we are holy in Him. We are the possession of God because we are in Christ, who is God's own Son. We walk in the light because we are in Him who is light itself. We have received compassion from God because Jesus Christ died for us and God loves us in Christ. And we proclaim His excellencies through the power of the Holy Spirit (Acts 1:4-8).

Ephesians 1:3 says, "Blessed be the God and Father of our Lord Jesus Christ, who has blessed us with every spiritual blessing . . . in Christ." We can look around us and see only a motley bunch of erstwhile sinners who deserve eternal damnation, but because we are in Christ we have been granted incredible spiritual privileges. Therefore we should be eternally grateful.

Focusing on the Facts

1. What did Peter mean when he described Christians as a "holy nation" (see pp. 83-84)?
2. To whom had God referred in the past as a holy nation (see p. 83)?
3. Who are God's unique new people (see p. 84)?
4. Holiness means that we have been ____ _____ unto God (see p. 84).
5. What is positional sanctification (see pp. 85-86)?
6. What change occurs in progressive sanctification (see p. 86)?
7. Why is sin a disaster in the life of a Christian (see p. 87)?
8. What does practical sanctification involve (see p. 88)?
9. When God spoke of a people of His own possession in the Old Testament, to whom was He referring (see p. 89)?

10. How was the church purchased, and to whom do all Christians belong (see p. 89)?
11. What is the darkness we have been called out of (see p. 90)?
12. What are two things that characterize that darkness (see p. 90)?
13. The unregenerate are both people in darkness and people _____ _____ (see p. 91)?
14. Why can it be said that Gentile Christians were once not a people (see p. 92)?
15. What two kinds of mercy does God extend to sinners (see pp. 92-93)?
16. Why does God extend mercy to sinners (see pp. 93-94)?
17. What meanings are associated with the word translated "proclaim" in verse 9 (see p. 95)?
18. What are Christians to proclaim (see p. 95)?
19. For what reason has God gifted us with the privileges Peter enumerated in 1 Peter 2:4-10 (see p. 96)?

Pondering the Principles

1. In the church today the need for personal and corporate holiness is often downplayed. Sin in the body of believers is considered by many to be the norm. David said that "the Lord examines the righteous, but the wicked and those who love violence his soul hates" (Ps. 11:5, NIV). More than one hundred years ago the Anglican bishop J. C. Ryle wrote, "A right knowledge of sin lies at the root of all saving Christianity. Without it such doctrines as justification, conversion, [and] sanctification, are 'words and names' which convey no meaning to the mind" (Holiness: Its Nature, Hindrances, Difficulties, and Roots [Welwyn: Evangelical Press, 1984 reprint], p. 1). Do you have God's perspective of sin—that it is a horror, a disaster, and something to be hated?

2. Our study of the good position and privileges we enjoy affirms that our God is good. Thomas Watson wrote, "God is the quintessence of all good things, He is superlatively good. The soul seeing a super-eminency in God, and admiring in Him that constellation of all excellencies, is carried out in love to Him in the highest degree. The measure of our love to God . . . must be to love Him without measure" (All Things for Good [Edinburgh:

Banner of Truth, 1986 reprint], p. 71). As you reflect on God's goodness to you, pray that He will increase your love for Him that you may be more closely bound to Him.

Scripture Index

Topical Index

Access to God. *See* God, access to

Affection for Christ. *See* Jesus Christ, affection for

Asceticism, problem with, 87-88

Bolton, Samuel, on spiritual duties, 51

Brooks, Thomas
on affection for Christ, 65
on spiritual duties, 51

Christianity
cost of. *See* Discipleship, cost of
uniqueness of, 16-17, 24-25

Church, the temple of God, 17-21

Compassion. *See* Mercy

Cornerstone, the. *See* Jesus Christ

Cost of discipleship. *See* Discipleship

Darkness. *See* Illumination

Depravity. *See* Man

Disappointment, freedom from, 56-60

Discipleship, cost of, 68-69

Dominion. *See* Priesthood, believers'

Duties, spiritual, 51, 68. *See also* Sacrifice, spiritual

Edwards, Jonathan, on the goodness of God, 65

Election
effects of the doctrine of, 74-75, 78-79, 96
foreknowledge and, 71-73

Jesus', 73-74
truth of, 70-75

Evangelism
definition of, 95
privilege of, 95-96
purpose of, 95
spiritual sacrifice of, 49

Evil, problem of. *See* God, goodness of

Externalism. *See* Legalism

Foreknowledge. *See* Election

Giving, importance of, 47-49

God
access to, 23-51, 55, 96
attributes of, 46-47
compassion of. *See* Mercy
goodness of, 54-55, 65, 97-98
fairness of, 54
lovingkindness of. *See* Mercy
mercy of. *See* Mercy
possession of. *See* Possession

Greatness, determining, 14-16

Heaven, reigning in. *See* Priesthood, believers'

Holiness
definition of, 84
means of, 84-85
Old Testament precedent, 83-84
progression of. *See* Sanctification

Illumination, darkness and, 90-91

Israel, apostasy of, 83-84. *See also* Jesus Christ, rejection of

Jesus Christ
  affection for, 60-65, 96
  cornerstone, the, 11-16,
    56-60, 65
  election of. *See* Election
  evaluating, 15-16
  love for. *See* affection for
  rejection of, 12-16, 61-64. *See
    also* Israel, apostasy of
  security in, 56-60, 96
  stone, the. *See* cornerstone,
    the
  trustworthiness of. *See* securi-
    ty in
  union with, 16-21, 96
Judaism. *See* Israel

Kaleidoscope of privileges. *See*
    Privileges, Christian

Legalism, problem with, 87-88
Lenski, R. C. H., on the stone of
    stumbling, 63
Levi, tribe of, 27. *See also*
    Priesthood
Louvre museum, illustration of
    judging paintings, 14
Lovingkindness. *See* Mercy

Man, depravity of, 78-79, 97
Mercy
  general, 92
  God's, 91-96
  special, 93-95
Ministry. *See* Priesthood
Monasticism. *See* Asceticism

Nadab and Abihu, death of, 34
Non-Christians, characteristics
    of, 90-91

Paul, writing style of, 8
Peter, writing style of, 8
Pharisees, legalism of the, 88

Pink, A. W., on God's mercy,
    94
Possession, God's, 89-90, 96
Praise, 46-47
Prayer, spiritual sacrifice of, 49
Priesthood
  believers', 23-51, 75-79
  Old Testament, 25-37, 43
  royal, 75-77, 79, 96
Privileges, Christian
  affection for Christ. *See* Jesus
    Christ, affection for
  access to God. *See* God, ac-
    cess to
  compassion. *See* Mercy
  dominion. *See* Priesthood,
    believers'
  duty contrasted with, 68-69,
    82-83
  election. *See* Election
  gratitude for, 96
  joy of, 8
  illumination. *See* Illumination
  illustration of, 8-9
  kaleidoscope of, 8-9
  meaning of, 8
  possession. *See* Possession
  proclamation. *See* Evangelism
  recipients of, 9-11
  security in Christ. *See* Jesus
    Christ, security in
  separation. *See* Holiness
  union with Christ. *See* Jesus
    Christ, union with
Proclamation. *See* Evangelism

Rejection of Christ. *See* Jesus
    Christ, rejection of
Religion, uniqueness of the
    Christian. *See*
    Christianity
Resources in Christ. *See* Privi-
    leges, Christian
Responsibilities. *See* Duties

Ryle, J. C., on the doctrine of human depravity, 78-79, 97

Sacrifices
  animal, 29-31, 33, 43
  spiritual, 43-51
Sanctification
  positional, 85-86
  practical, 87-89
  progressive, 85-87
  See also Holiness
Security, in Christ. *See* Jesus Christ
Separation. *See* Holiness, Sanctification
Sharing. *See* Giving
Sin
  God's view of, 97
  man's. *See* Man
Spurgeon, Charles Haddon, on being one with Christ, 20
Stoicism, problem with, 88

Stone, the. *See* Jesus Christ
Suffering, problem of. *See* God, goodness of

Temple, the church and the. *See* Church

Union with Christ. *See* Jesus Christ, union with
Unregenerate, the. *See* Non-Christians

Watson, Thomas
  on the goodness of God, 97-98
  on hypocrisy, 38-39
  on the indwelling Christ, 20-21
  on nearness to God, 38
  on the rock of God, 65
World, corrupt evaluations of the, 15-16
Worship. *See* Praise